BEHIND HER SMILE WAS PAIN

BEHIND HER SMILE WAS PAIN

CYMONE ADAMS

TyneBell Publishing

BEHIND HER SMILE IT WAS PAIN

A NOVEL BY CYMONE ADAMS

PUBLISHED BY TYNE BELL PUBLISHING

Follow Us!

BE SURE TO FOLLOW AUTHOR FOR UPDATES AND NEW RELEASES!

FACEBOOK: CYMONE ADAMS

ALSO CHECK OUT MY MOBILEBAR PAGE ON INSTAGRAM: @1220MIXUP !!!!

TO SUBMIT A MANUSCRIPT FOR OUR REVIEW EMAIL US AT

TYNEBPUB@GMAIL.COM

FOLLOW US:

IG: @TYNEBELLPUB/ @TALKTOEMSHAN

EDITOR: T. JONES

COVER CREDIT: AMONE ALLISON

IG: @AMONEEE_

Forward

TO THE YOUNG TEENAGE CYMONE

FROM THE YOUNG QUEEN WHO HAS BATTLED
HERSELF THROUGHOUT THE YEARS

TO THE YOUNG QUEEN WHO FOUGHT TOOTH
AND NAIL TO SEE THIS PROJECT THROUGH...
PAT YOURSELF ON THE BACK LOVE.

WE FACE A LOT OF BATTLES THAT ARE IN
SILENCE. WE HAVE TO FACE THESE IN MOST
CASES, NOT BY CHOICE. YOU CHOSE TO
TACKLE THIS AT THE HEIGHT OF YOUR
GRIND. THERE ARE NO TOUGHER BATTLES
THAN THE INTERNAL ONES.

THESE ARE USUALLY THE HARDEST BECAUSE
IT REQUIRES A VERSION OF OURSELVES THAT
WE DON'T LIKE. THIS VERSION OF US HAS TO
BE VULNERABLE. THE PROBLEM WITH THAT IS
STRONG WOMEN VIEW VULNERABILITY AS A
WEAKNESS. WELL, I AM HERE TO TELL YOU

THAT THIS TRANSPARENCY WILL ONLY MAKE YOU STRONGER.

THANK YOU FOR LIVING YOUR LIFE ON YOUR TERMS AND SHOWING US WHAT A REAL WALK WITH GOD LOOKS LIKE.

IMPERFECT, HONEST, AND IMPULSIVE BUT ALWAYS OPEN TO CORRECTION AND GOD'S GUIDANCE. TRUST THAT AT A LOT OF MOMENTS WE MAY NOT KNOW WHAT OR WHERE TO GO BUT WE KNOW HE HAS US AT THE END OF THE DAY.

I PRAY YOUR STORY IMPACTS EVERYONE THAT READS IT AND THAT THEY KNOW IT'S NOT ABOUT HOW THE JOURNEY STARTS, IT'S ONLY ABOUT WHAT YOU DO TO SURVIVE IT.

ENJOY THIS MOMENT. IT'S BEEN WAITING FOR YOUR ARRIVAL FOR A WHILE.

-S. TOLBERT

Acknowledgements

I CAN DO ALL THINGS THROUGH CHRIST WHO STRENGTHENS ME. THANK YOU, GOD, FOR BEING WITH ME EVERY STEP OF THE WAY. NOTHING WOULD'VE BEEN POSSIBLE WITHOUT YOU. GOD THANKS FOR GIVING ME THE GIFT TO INSPIRE AND MOTIVATE MY READERS THROUGH MY WORDS.

I WANT TO THANK TYNEBELL PUBLISHING FOR THE SUPPORT AND FOR HELPING ME PUSH THROUGH TO COMPLETE THIS BOOK.

TO MY MOM CHANEL (MARIE) I CAN'T THANK YOU ENOUGH FOR BEING MY MOM AND JUST BEING YOU. THANKS FOR MOLDING ME TO STAND ON MY OWN AND NEVER GIVE UP.

TO MY SISTER CHANTELLE (MADDIE) THANKS FOR BEING EVERYTHING A SISTER NEEDS. IF IT ALL FAILS I KNOW YOU GOT ME AND MY BOYS

TO MY FAMILY AND FRIENDS, THANKS FOR SUPPORTING AND BELIEVING IN ME. YOU GUYS MOTIVATE ME TO GO EVEN HARDER. I'M FOREVER GRATEFUL AND THANKFUL FOR ALL MY READERS

-AUTHOR CYMONE ADAMS

I

Mone's World

MANY WILL START FAST, BUT FEW WILL FINISH STRONG - GARY RYAN BLAIR

MONE'S WORLD

I GO BY THE NAME MONE. MANY PEOPLE CALL ME BIG MONE... HEAVY ON THE BIG. I WAS BORN TO MARIE AND C-JAY. RAISED IN THE STREETS OF DETROIT, THE "WESTSIDE" OF SEVEN MILE TO BE EXACT. I'M THE SECOND OLDEST OF FIVE CHILDREN. CHO, MYSELF, MADDIE, GOOSE, AND MOOK. WE LIVED IN A FULL HOUSE- FAMILY MEMBERS OF EVERY GENERATION. THERE WERE MY GREAT GRANDPARENTS (POP & GRANDMA), GRANDPARENTS (CAT & LARRY), MARIE, AUNTIE(KASH), UNCLE(WHYTE), MY SIBLINGS, AND MYSELF. ALL OF US WERE DEEP IN A THREE-BEDROOM HOME SO YOU CAN JUST IMAGINE HOW INTERESTING MOST DAYS WERE. DIFFERENT GENERATIONS, AND DIFFERENT PERSONALITIES BUT NEVER A DULL MOMENT. FROM FIGHTING AND ARGUING ON HOLIDAYS AND BIRTHDAYS TO JUST LEARNING TO APPRECIATE THE FACT WE HAD EACH OTHER. POP AND GRANDMA CARED FOR EVERYONE THE BEST THEY COULD. WE WENT TO THEM FOR EVERYTHING. GRANDMA EVEN KEPT US IN THE MOST FLY K-MART GEAR, OR WHATEVER SHE COULD FIND ON THE CLEARANCE RACK AT HUDSON. BOY, DID I HATE THOSE TWO-PIECE SWEATSUITS WITH THE K-MART ZIP-UP BOOTS? I WAS WARM BUT I WAS EMBARRASSED ABOUT THE LOOK. THAT'S ALL SHE COULD AFFORD

FOR THE FIVE OF US. BUT SHE MADE SURE WE NEVER WENT WITHOUT.

I WAS ALWAYS THE ODD ONE OUT OF EVERYONE. I WAS THE ONE WHO GOT TEASED AROUND THE HOUSE THE MOST. I WAS THE DARKEST AND BIGGEST ONE OUT OF THE BUNCH. CHO AND WHYTE WOULD FLAME ME. I HATED IT BECAUSE I NEVER KNEW HOW TO ROAST THEM BACK. I WOULD RUN TO GRANDMA CAT AND TELL HER WHAT THEY WERE SAYING ABOUT ME. CAT ALWAYS REMINDED ME TO NEVER LET THOSE WORDS BREAK ME. SHE COULD RELATE BECAUSE SHE WAS ON THE HEAVY SIDE AS A KID TOO. COMING FROM THIS TYPE OF BACKGROUND TRULY ESTABLISHED MY STRENGTHS AND GRATEFULNESS FOR EVERYTHING LATER ON IN LIFE. MY FAMILY WAS VERY DYSFUNCTIONAL. BUT WHOSE FAMILY ISN'T?

OUR HOUSE NOT ONLY STOOD AS A PILLAR FOR MY FAMILY AND MADE SURE WE ALL HAD A ROOF OVER OUR HEADS BUT WAS ALSO VERY MUCH THE PARTY HOUSE. EVERYBODY KNEW THEY COULD PULL UP AND SOMEONE WOULD BE THERE. IF YOU HAVE EVER PLAYED THE GAME 'FREEZE TAG' THINK OF WHEN YOU HAVE A PLACE THAT STANDS FOR GLUE. GLUE IS A REPRESENTATION OF A SAFE PLACE. IF

YOU GET THERE, WHATEVER IS CHASING YOU,
THAT'S WHERE YOU CAN COME AND FOR SURE
BE SAFE. SOMETIMES MULTIPLE PEOPLE THAT
ARE PLAYING MAKE IT TO GLUE AT THE SAME
TIME. THEN GLUE BECOMES CROWDED. BUT
EVEN WITH IT BEING CROWDED IT'S STILL A
SAFE PLACE. THAT'S WHAT OUR HOUSE WAS
LIKE TO A LOT OF PEOPLE. UNFORTUNATELY,
ALL THAT CHANGED WHEN POP AND
GRANDMA GOT SICK AND PASSED AWAY FROM
CANCER. I HAD TO BE ABOUT FIFTEEN YEARS
OLD WHEN THIS HAPPENED. THEY WERE
REALLY MY FIRST CLOSE FAMILY LOSSES. I
REALLY DIDN'T KNOW THE REAL MEANING OF
DEATH OR WHAT TO EXPECT. ALL I KNEW WAS
SOME FACES THAT I WAS USED TO SEEING
EVERY DAY WERE NO LONGER HERE. I DIDN'T
REALIZE THE DRAMA THAT CAN FOLLOW
WHEN ELDERS IN THE FAMILY START PASSING
AWAY. EVEN IF IT WASN'T THE DRAMA IT STILL
WAS MAJOR CHANGES THAT WERE TAKING
PLACE. IN MY GREAT GRANDPARENTS' WILL,
MARIE WAS LEFT WITH THE HOUSE AND CARS.
POP AND GRANDMA ESTABLISHED "ORDER"
AND THEY DID THINGS A CERTAIN WAY FOR A
LONG TIME AND WHEN ALL THOSE
GENERATIONS ARE UNDER ONE ROOF, OF
COURSE, EVERYONE CATCHES ON TO THE
"ORDER" THEY SET. ALL OF THAT DISAPPEARED
AFTER THEIR DEATHS.

MY "BLISSFUL " LIFE WAS JUST BEGINNING. I WAS DEALING WITH THE THINGS THAT CAME WITH BEING A TEENAGER, BUT I WAS ALSO EXPERIENCING MY FIRST SORROW OF TWO PEOPLE I LOVED AND WHO WERE NO LONGER AROUND. THESE TRANSITIONS ARE HARD ON ANYBODY AND EVEN HARDER ON A YOUNG TEEN WHO IS STARTING TO FIGURE OUT THEIR OWN LIFE. WITH ALL THE THINGS THAT WERE GOING ON AROUND THE HOUSE MY EXPOSURE GREW, WHICH MEANS THAT MY CURIOSITY GREW AS WELL. THESE THINGS LED ME TO A PATH I WOULD CONTINUE TO FOLLOW THROUGHOUT MY EARLY ADULTHOOD. THAT LACK OF STRUCTURE MADE IT POSSIBLE FOR THE STREETS TO BEGIN TO MOLD ME.

2

What Turned me to the Streets

"GUIDANCE? I NEVER HAD THAT, STREETS WAS MY SECOND HOME

WELCOMED ME WITH OPEN ARMS AND PROVIDED A PLACE TO CRASH AT..."- JAY-Z

OUR HOUSE REALLY BECAME THE TURN-UP HOUSE. OH, IT WENT DOWN ON SORRENTO STREET. I'M JUST GONNA SAY MARIE IS THE PARTY QUEEN AND SHE KNOWS EVERYBODY. MARIE PARTIED SO MUCH THAT THEY STARTED NAMING OUR HOUSE "O'SO CRISPY", A WHOLE AFTER-HOUR CLUB NAME. A NAME SHE, MY AUNT KASH, AND THEIR FRIENDS CAME UP WITH. THEY ALL WOULD MEET AT OUR HOUSE AFTER THE CLUB. THEY WOULD PARTY UNTIL THE SUN CAME UP. SOME OF THEIR FRIENDS NEVER LEFT UNTIL THE NEXT AFTERNOON. THERE USED TO BE A LOT OF BIG SMOKE-OUTS AND DICE GAMES. THEY EVEN TURNED THE DINING ROOM INTO A STUDIO ONCE UPON A TIME. IF YOU KNOW THERE'S A LOT OF PARTYING THEN YOU KNOW BILLS WEREN'T GETTING PAID. I DON'T EVEN THINK MARIE KNEW WHAT A BILL WAS UNTIL MY GREAT-GRANDPARENTS PASSED. EVEN THOUGH THEY MADE THE DECISION TO LEAVE THE HOUSE WITH MARIE, SHE DEFINITELY WASN'T PREPARED TO TAKE OVER AND BE THE HEAD OF EVERYTHING. ON TOP OF THE PARTYING EVERY DAY, MARIE LET ANYBODY STAY WITH US. YOU COULD COME TO HANG OUT FRIDAY NIGHT AND STAY THE WEEKEND. MOST OF CHO AND WHYTE'S FRIENDS FROM THE NEIGHBORHOOD MOVED IN WITH US. AFTER A WHILE DUE TO ALL THESE DIFFERENT PEOPLE IN THE HOUSE, IT BECAME NOWHERE

TO SLEEP. EVERYBODY REALLY SLEPT
WHEREVER THEY FELL ASLEEP.

A COUPLE OF THEIR FRIENDS USED TO FLIRT
WITH ME. BUT AT THE SAME TIME, THEY WERE
SNEAKING AND MESSING AROUND WITH MARIE
BECAUSE THEY NEEDED A PLACE TO STAY. SO
NOW MARIE IS STARTING TO TURN ON ME AND
CRITICIZE ME FOR BEING IN THEIR FACE.
THERE WAS A LOT OF TENSION IN THE HOUSE.
I REALLY HAD NO CLUE AT FIRST SHE WAS
SNEAKING AROUND WITH THIS ONE
PARTICULAR BOY. I WAS AT AN AGE WHERE I
WAS LIKING BOYS, BUT IT WAS MORE SO THE
BOYS WERE COMING ON TO ME. DON'T GET ME
WRONG, I WAS A LITTLE CURIOUS, BUT I
DIDN'T FALL INTO THOSE BOYS' TRAPS. MARIE
TAKING IT OUT ON ME AND SWITCHING UP ON
ME ABOUT THESE RANDOMS MADE ME FEEL A
CERTAIN WAY ABOUT HER. I STARTED
SHOWING A LACK OF RESPECT FOR HER. I FELT
LIKE I WAS LEFT TO FEND FOR MYSELF. I WAS
LEARNING A HARD LESSON FROM MY OWN
MOTHER. ONCE THAT DRAMA AND HOUSE
FULL OF PEOPLE BEGAN TO BE THE EVERYDAY
SCENE, THINGS GOT A LITTLE BIT TOO
UNCOMFORTABLE FOR ME. OUR HOME WAS
NOW GOING DOWNHILL. I STARTED TRYING TO
DISTANCE MYSELF FROM THE HOUSE. I WAS
ALREADY HAVING MY ISSUES WITH MARIE AND

THEN IT FELT LIKE THERE WAS NO ROOM FOR ME IN THE PLACE I CALLED HOME. THAT FORCED ME TO START TRYING TO FIND COMFORT OUTSIDE OF HOME. ALL OF THIS WAS BUILDING ME AND BREAKING ME AT THE SAME TIME. I WAS TRYING TO FIGURE OUT HOW TO GROW IN THAT TYPE OF ENVIRONMENT THAT WAS BUILT TO STUNT MY GROWTH. EVEN THOUGH I WAS YOUNG I WAS TRYING TO PROCESS EVERYTHING THAT WAS GOING ON AROUND ME.

3

Loyalty Caused Pain

"SOME PEOPLE AREN'T LOYAL TO YOU... THEY ARE LOYAL TO THEIR NEED OF YOU... ONCE THEIR NEEDS CHANGE, SO DOES THEIR LOYALTY"- UNKNOWN

I TRIED STAYING OUT AS MUCH AS I COULD. STAYING AWAY ALLOWED ME TO BUILD BONDS WITH OTHER PEOPLE AND LEARN WHO I WAS OUTSIDE OF MY CROWDED LIVING SITUATION. I HUNG OUT WITH THESE TWO GIRLS, KELSEY AND BRIE. WE HUNG LIKE WET CLOTHES. WE WERE LITERALLY CONNECTED AT THE HIPS. WE WENT TO SCHOOL TOGETHER, SKATING, AND EVEN POPPED INTO ALL THE NEIGHBORHOOD PARTIES. JUST KNOW IF YOU SAW THEM, I WASN'T TOO FAR BEHIND. KELSEY AND I WOULD WALK AND DANCE IN THE STREET UNTIL THE STREETLIGHTS TURNED ON. I WOULD ALWAYS STAY OUT ALL DAY SO I COULD SPEND THE NIGHT AT ONE OF THEIR HOUSES. KELSEY'S MOMMA GOT TO THE POINT WHERE SHE WAS TIRED OF ME ASKING TO SPEND THE NIGHT. SHE WOULD SAY "SHE CAN COME OVER BUT SHE CAN'T SPEND A NIGHT". KELSEY KNEW I DIDN'T WANT TO GO HOME SO SHE WOULD SNEAK ME IN SOME NIGHTS. I WOULD HAVE TO SLEEP BEHIND HER COUCH JUST SO HER MOMMA WOULDN'T CATCH ME. IT'S CRAZY TO THINK NOW THAT I WOULD RATHER STAY AT SOMEONE ELSE'S HOUSE UNDER THESE TYPES OF CONDITIONS RATHER THAN JUST GO HOME AND DEAL WITH EVERYTHING THAT WAS GOING ON THERE.

KELSEY AND I FOUND OURSELVES LIKING

THESE OLDER BOYS IN THE HOOD. THEY ALSO HAPPENED TO BE MY UNCLE WHYTE'S FRIENDS. WE WERE JUST BEING FAST. WHEN YOU SEE DUDES LIVING LIFE, GETTING MONEY, AND FINE, AS A YOUNG GIRL THAT IS SUPER APPEALING TO YOU. IT WAS EXCITING BEING ABLE TO BE INVOLVED IN THESE DUDES' LIVES. BUT WHAT WE DIDN'T REALIZE IS ALL OF THE STUFF THAT COMES WITH MESSING WITH THESE TYPES OF DUDES. EVERY TIME ONE OF THEM WOULD RIDE DOWN THE STREET WE WOULD STOP THEIR CARS ASKING THEM TO TAKE US TO THE STORE OR TO GIVE US SOME MONEY. THEY STOPPED EVERY TIME AND GAVE US WHAT WE WANTED.

IT WAS THIS ONE GUY WHOSE NAME WAS "JUAN". IT WAS SOMETHING ABOUT HIM THAT I LOVED. HE HAD MONEY AND ALL THE OLD-SCHOOL CARS WITH RIMS THAT WERE BIGGER THAN ME. I GUESS THIS IS WHY I LIKE OLD-SCHOOL CARS NOW. HIS FLASHY ATTIRE WAS ALSO A PLUS. BUT I DEFINITELY STOPPED WHATEVER I WAS DOING WHEN I SAW HIM COMING UP THE STREET. JUAN WOULD HAVE ME BLUSHING EVERY TIME I WALKED AWAY FROM HIS CAR. EVENTUALLY, WE STARTED MESSING AROUND. HE BECAME MY FIRST. HE TOOK A SISTER SOUL. WE WERE OF COURSE SNEAKING AROUND THOUGH BECAUSE I

WASN'T OLD ENOUGH. KELSEY AND I WOULD
GET DRESSED AND SNEAK TO THE CORNER TO
MEET UP WITH JUAN AND HIS BOY MARK
EVERY CHANCE WE GOT. THE FOUR OF US
RODE AROUND THAT WHOLE SUMMER
BANGING THAT JEEZY THUG MOTIVATION 101
CD. ON THIS ONE PARTICULAR DAY, WE
BROUGHT BRIE ALONG WITH US TO RIDE WITH
JUAN. WE WERE ON OUR WAY TO GET MARK
AND SOMEHOW HIS CAR STARTED GIVING US
PROBLEMS AND BREAKING DOWN ON US AND
BOY WAS I PISSED. WE WERE A BLOCK AWAY
FROM THESE GIRLS WE HAD BEEF WITH. WE
HAD JUST FOUGHT A COUPLE OF THEM
EARLIER THAT WEEK SO THE BEEF WAS STILL
SUPER FRESH. JUST LIKE WHEN YOU WALK
INTO A ROOM WITH SOMEONE YOU DON'T
LIKE. BEING IN SOMEBODY'S NEIGHBORHOOD
YOU DON'T LIKE FEELS THE SAME WAY. YOU
START BEING ON HIGH ALERT AND GET SUPER
IRRITATED ESPECIALLY WHEN THINGS ARE
OUT OF YOUR CONTROL.

I RESEMBLED A LADY THAT DAY. I WAS SUPER
CUTE, I HAD ON A NICE OUTFIT, MY HAIR DID,
AND EVERYTHING. LOOKING LIKE THAT ONE. I
WAS WAY TOO CUTE TO BE FIGHTING. I JUST
REMEMBER HOPING WE DON'T SEE THESE
GIRLS. NOW TRUST AND BELIEVE I WASN'T
HOPING WE DIDN'T SEE THESE GIRLS OUT OF

FEAR. I JUST WANTED TO REMAIN CUTE FOR
THE REST OF THE DAY, ESPECIALLY SINCE I
WAS HANGING WITH MY BOO. JUAN WAS OUT
OF THE CAR FOR LIKE TWENTY MINUTES
TRYING TO GET THE CAR STARTED. THE
LONGER HIS CAR STAYED DOWN THE MORE
IRRITATED I GOT. WHILE HE WAS IN FRONT OF
THE CAR LOOKING UNDER THE HOOD HERE
COME SOME OF THOSE GIRLS RIDING UP THE
STREET. ONCE THEY SAW HIM THEY STOPPED
TO TALK. THEN THEY REALIZED IT WAS US
SITTING IN THE CAR SO THEY STARTED
TALKING BIG SMACK GETTING ON TIP. I
IGNORED THEM AS LONG AS I COULD. I
STARTED QUESTIONING AND SNAPPING AT
JUAN CUZ I FELT LIKE HE SET US UP. THINGS
JUST DIDN'T SEEM RIGHT. EVERYTHING JUST
FELT OUTTA PLACE.

OF COURSE, HE IS LIKE, "MAN THEY AIN'T
GONNA TOUCH YOU". HE TRIED TO GET THE
CAR STARTED FAST AND AT THE SAME TIME HE
KEPT TELLING THE GIRLS TO "GONE HEAD ON.
KEEP IT MOVING!!". THEY WERE STILL TALKING
CRAZY AS THEY PULLED OFF. I TELL HIM TO
HURRY UP AND GET THIS CAR STARTED. IF HE
DIDN'T HURRY UP I WOULD JUST WALK. I WAS
SO FED UP WITH HIM AND HIS CAR WASN'T
MAKING THE SITUATION MUCH BETTER. AS I'M
SITTING THERE FOR TEN MORE MINUTES. I SEE

THE GIRLS WALKING UP THE STREET AND IT'S LIKE SEVEN OF THEM NOW. THREE OF THEM WERE COMING FROM ONE WAY AND THE OTHERS WERE COMING FROM THE OTHER END OF THE BLOCK. I TURNED AROUND AND ASKED KELSEY AND BRIE IF THEY WERE READY CAUSE I KNEW IT WAS ABOUT TO GO DOWN. BRIE WAS PREGNANT WITH MY NEPHEW AT THE TIME. BUT THAT DIDN'T STOP ANYTHING BECAUSE WE HAD BEEN FIGHTING ALL WEEK, PREGNANT AND ALL. SO THE GIRLS HYPED THIS ONE GIRL UP TO COME HIT ME BUT SHE WAS SCARED. AS I'M SITTING IN THE FRONT SEAT, ONE OF THE GIRLS WALKS UP TO THE CAR AND SPITS ON ME. I GOT OUT OF THE CAR AND WENT CRAZY IMMEDIATELY. SO NOW SOMEHOW I'M FIGHTING LIKE THREE GIRLS AT ONCE. SOME OF THEM WERE GROWN WOMEN BUT THEY COULDN'T GET ME TO THE GROUND. I'M FIGHTING FOR MY LIFE JUST SWINGING. ALL I KNOW IS THAT JUAN WAS TRYING TO BREAK IT UP. HE FINALLY GOT THEM UP OFF ME AND IT WAS JUST A LOT GOING ON. IT SEEMED LIKE IT WAS PEOPLE WATCHING FROM EVERYWHERE. I WAS SO HEATED. I STRIKE OUT AND START WALKING HOME, BRIE AND KELSEY FOLLOW. AS WE WALKED, KELSEY WAS LIKE "YOU BLEEDING BAD MONE". I LOOK DOWN AND I JUST SEE A WHOLE BUNCH OF BLOOD ON MY SHIRT BUT I DON'T KNOW WHERE THE BLOOD IS COMING FROM. WE STOPPED TO TRY TO FIGURE OUT

WHERE IT WAS COMING FROM AND REALIZED I
HAD A BIG CUT DOWN TO THE WHITE MEAT
ON THE RIGHT SIDE OF MY STOMACH. I DIDN'T
FEEL THE PAIN BECAUSE I WAS SO MAD AND
MY ADRENALINE WAS RUSHING. I ENDED UP
HAVING TO GET TWENTY-TWO STAPLES TO
CLOSE THE CUT UP.

AS WE WALKED HOME WE TOLD OUR SIDES OF
THE FIGHT, KELSEY LIKE, "I COULDN'T DO
MUCH BECAUSE I AIN'T GET OUT THE CAR
FAST ENOUGH". OF COURSE, I'M TELLING MY
END AND WHAT I CAN RECALL FROM THE
SITUATION, BUT I HAD PEEPED SOMETHING
WHILE WE WERE TALKING. BRIE WAS A LITTLE
TOO QUIET AS WE WERE TALKING. SO ME
BEING WHO I AM I ASKED STRAIGHT UP,
KNOWING IN MY HEAD THE ANSWER THAT
WAS ABOUT TO COME OUT OF THIS GIRL'S
MOUTH. I'M LIKE "HOW MANY GIRLS WERE
YOU FIGHTING, BRIE "? SHE AIN'T SAYING
ANYTHING SO NOW I'M REALLY PISSED. I JUST
STARTED GOING OFF AGAIN. LIKE, "HOW YOU
AIN'T HELP US FIGHT?!" I STARTED POWER
WALKING TRYING TO GET HOME. WE FINALLY
MADE IT TO MY HOUSE. EVERYBODY WAS OVER
THERE AND I'M TELLING MARIE WHAT
HAPPENED. HER AND MY AUNT KASH WENT
CRAZY. THEY SAW ALL THAT DAMN BLOOD
AND HEARD HOW THE WHOLE SITUATION

PLAYED OUT SO THEY WERE READY TO SLIDE
BACK OVER THERE. WE PULLED BACK OVER
THERE THREE CARS DEEP. MARIE MADE ALL OF
US FIGHT AGAIN. KELSEY AND BRIE FOUGHT
THIS TIME AND THAT'S WHEN MY CUT RIPPED
OPEN EVEN BIGGER. THE SAME GIRLS WANTED
REVENGE DAYS LATER. THEY PULLED DOWN ON
US IN FRONT OF MY UNCLE BOOM'S HOUSE.
THE WHOLE HOOD WAS OUT THERE THAT DAY.
WE WERE OUT THERE LISTENING TO MUSIC
PLAYING IN THE STREETS. I SAW THEM RIDING
UP AND DOWN THE BLOCK, BY THE THIRD
TIME THEY RODE PAST, I CALLED MARIE. SHE
PULLED UP FAST WITH MY COUSIN AND
WHOEVER WAS AT THE HOUSE WITH HER AND
HOPPED OUT ON TIP. THE GIRLS SAW HER AND
GOT SCARED. ONE GIRL GOT BACK IN THE CAR
AND DROVE THROUGH THE CROWD AND RAN
MARIE OVER, I SPAZZED OUT ON THEM AFTER
THAT. IT TOOK THE WHOLE HOOD TO BREAK
THAT FIGHT UP. CAT BEAT ME WITH A RADIO
WIRE BECAUSE SHE SAID IT WAS MY FAULT
MARIE GOT RAN OVER. I DIDN'T CARE EVERY
CHANCE I GOT, I TORTURED THEM, GIRLS. I
KNOW MOST PEOPLE HAVE SEEN THE SHOW,
TOM AND JERRY. WELL, THAT'S HOW IT WAS
WITH US THE WHOLE SUMMER...ON SIGHT!
EVERY TIME I WOULD CATCH ONE OF THEM
GIRLS THEY WOULD RUN IF THEY WEREN'T ALL
TOGETHER. THEY WERE ALL OLDER THAN ME
AND NEVER COULD GO ONE ON ONE WITH ME,

OR THEY NEVER WANTED TO. UNTIL THIS DAY I REALLY DON'T KNOW WHAT THE BEEF WAS ABOUT OR HOW IT CAME ABOUT. BUT I DO KNOW THE WHOLE HOOD KNEW THEY COULD CALL ME TO BEAT ANYBODY UP AFTER THAT SUMMER. CHO AND UNCLE WHYTE ALWAYS CALLED ME EVERY TIME THEY HAD A PROBLEM WITH ANY GIRL.

THOSE BRAWLS SHOWED ME SOME STUFF. THEY SHOWED ME FIRST THINGS FIRST I HAD HANDS. BUT THEY ALSO SHOWED ME THAT MAYBE KELSEY AND BRIE WEREN'T AS MUCH OF A FRIEND OF MINE AS I THOUGHT THEY WERE. LOOKING BACK WE WERE YOUNG AND RECKLESS BUT THERE'S JUST CERTAIN STUFF YOU DON'T DO. YOU DON'T LEAVE A GUNFIGHT WITH A FULL CLIP AND YOU NEVER LET YOUR PEOPLE BATTLE ALONE. EVEN IF YOU DON'T WANNA FIGHT YOU BETTER FIGURE OUT HOW TO KEEP THEM UP OFF YOUR PEOPLE. AIN'T NO BEING THERE FOR THE FIGHT AND DON'T THROW ANY PUNCHES. THIS KIND OF STUFF IS A RECIPE FOR ME TO HAVE TO PUT MY HANDS ON YOU MYSELF WHEN WE GET AWAY FROM THE SITUATION.

MY BOND WITH KELSEY AND BRIE CHANGED AFTER THAT. THAT WAS MY FIRST LESSON ON LOYALTY. I WAS TOO YOUNG TO KNOW WHAT LOYALTY WAS BUT I KNEW THEY DIDN'T HAVE MY BACK THAT DAY. I WAS KIND OF HURT. THERE WERE STILL LITTLE SNAKE THINGS THAT WERE HAPPENING THAT I DIDN'T LIKE THAT KELSEY HAD DONE. BUT I NEVER SAID ANYTHING. CERTAIN THINGS YOU JUST DON'T LET GO DOWN WHEN SOMEBODY IS SUPPOSED TO BE YOUR BEST FRIEND. KELSEY WAS MY BEST FRIEND BUT FOR SOME REASON, I WASN'T HERS. NO MATTER WHAT A PERSON MEANS TO YOU DOESN'T MEAN THEY FEEL THE SAME WAY ABOUT YOU.

AS WE GOT OLDER, I STARTED REALIZING A LOT OF THE THINGS SHE DID IN OUR FRIENDSHIP JUST NEVER REALLY SAT RIGHT WITH ME. WE EVENTUALLY GREW APART. I FOUND MY OWN LANE. I HUNG WITH FEMALES THROUGHOUT SCHOOL BUT I NEVER GOT CLOSE ENOUGH TO CALL THEM MY BEST FRIEND. EVEN NOW I DON'T HAVE TOO MANY FRIENDS. I'VE BEEN CROSSED TOO OFTEN BY FEMALES. MY SISTER, MADDIE, IS EVERYTHING I NEED IN A FRIEND. SHE IS MY BEST FRIEND AND THAT'S BEEN WORKING JUST FINE FOR ME. AFTER I FELL BACK A LITTLE FROM BRIE AND KELSEY, I STARTED SEEKING

RELATIONSHIPS WITH GIRLS WHO WERE A
LITTLE OLDER THAN ME. MAYBE IT WAS ME
LOOKING FOR GUIDANCE? OR MAYBE I
THOUGHT OLDER PEOPLE UNDERSTOOD WHAT
MY IDEA OF LOYALTY WAS.

4

Curiosity

"ANY FOOL CAN KNOW...THE POINT IS TO UNDERSTAND"- ALBERT EINSTEIN

I STARTED HANGING OUT WITH THIS GIRL NAMED RUBY. SHE WAS OLDER THAN ME. SHE STAYED DOWN THE STREET FROM US. RUBY HAD ALL THE GUYS IT SEEMED LIKE. THEY WOULD PULL UP, GIVE HER GIFTS, AND MONEY AND THAT WOULD BE THAT. I USED TO SIT ON HER PORCH AND JUST WATCH HER. SHE HAD GUYS PULLING UP BACK TO BACK SOMETIMES AT THE SAME TIME. I STILL DON'T UNDERSTAND HOW SHE USED TO PULL IT OFF. I CAN LAUGH ABOUT IT NOW BECAUSE I KNOW SHE WAS PLAYING A REALLY DANGEROUS GAME WITH THEM GUYS. BUT WE WERE YOUNG AND SHE WAS LIVING LIFE. I REALLY THOUGHT RUBY WAS LIT. SHE HAD THIS FLASHY LIFESTYLE. RUBY WAS CUTE; SHE KEPT A CAR, AND A NEW HAIRSTYLE WEEKLY, AND STAYED IN THE MOST FLY CLOTHES. BUT EVEN WITH HER HAVING ALL THE DUDES I THINK WHAT ATTRACTED ME TO HER THE MOST WAS THAT SHE WAS A MONEY-MAKER. THAT DREW ME IN BECAUSE THAT'S WHAT I WANTED.... MONEY. I WOULD RUN DOWN TO RUBY'S HOUSE EVERY CHANCE I GOT. ONE OF OUR NOSEY NEIGHBORS WOULD WATCH US FROM HER TOP WINDOW. THE NEIGHBOR TRIED TELLING MARIE TO KEEP ME FROM DOWN THERE WITH RUBY BEFORE I ENDED UP PREGNANT. MARIE IGNORED HER AND I WAS STILL RUNNING DOWN THERE. I WAS WITH RUBY SO MUCH SHE GOT TIRED OF ME NOT BEING OLD ENOUGH TO

DO ANYTHING WITH HER. SO SHE GOT ME A
FAKE ID. SO NOW I'M LIT. I COULD GO TO
BARS, CLUBS, OR CASINOS. THE ID DIDN'T
LOOK ANYTHING LIKE ME BUT WE DECIDED TO
TRY IT OUT ANYWAY.

RUBY AND HER TWO GIRLFRIENDS PREPARED
ME ALL DAY TRYING TO PUT MAKEUP ON MY
FACE SO I COULD LOOK LIKE THE GIRL ON THE
ID. WE ENDED UP GOING TO ST. ANDREWS
NIGHT CLUB. RUBY TOLD ME TO GET IN LINE
AND GO AHEAD OF HER AND HER FRIENDS
AND IF I MADE IT IN, I WOULD WAIT IN THE
BATHROOM FOR HER. BUT IF I DIDN'T MAKE IT
I WOULD HAVE TO WAIT IN THE CAR ALL
NIGHT. I'M NERVOUS WALKING UP TO THE
BOUNCER. HE YELLS, "LADIES HAVE YOUR IDS
OUT." SO IT'S MY TURN I'M TRYING MY
HARDEST TO MAKE THE UGLY FACE OF THE
GIRL AND WALK SEXY IN THE HIGH HEELS I
HAD ON. HE GRABS THE ID BUT BARELY LOOKS
AT IT AND IS LIKE "GO AHEAD." IT WAS ON
FROM THERE. I SAW SOME OF MY UNCLE
WHYTE'S FRIENDS THERE. THEY COULDN'T
BELIEVE IT, THEY WERE READY TO BUST ME
OUT TO HIM. MAN, YOU COULDN'T TELL ME
ANYTHING, I REALLY STARTED FEELING
MYSELF. WE HAD A BALL THAT NIGHT. RUBY
WAS LIKE A BIG SISTER I NEVER HAD. SHE
SHOWED AN ALTERNATIVE WAY TO PLAY

THESE GAMES WHEN IT CAME TO MEN. I WAS ALL FOR HER ENCOURAGEMENT BECAUSE I LIKED WHERE SHE WAS COMING FROM. EVEN THOUGH SHE WAS WAY AHEAD OF THE GAME. I WAS TRYING TO KEEP UP WITH HER AND HANGING OUT WITH HER MADE ME FEEL GROWN. I LIKED THAT FEELING AND WAS DOING IT OUT OF CURIOSITY, BUT IN REALITY, I WASN'T AS READY FOR THAT LIFESTYLE AS I THOUGHT. RUDY AND I STILL REMAIN FRIENDS TO THIS DAY. SHE JUST CHOSE A DIFFERENT ROUTE THAN ME AND WAS DOING WHAT WAS BEST FOR HER. I HAD TO SLOW DOWN AND FIND MY OWN PATH. I'M NOT GONNA ACT AS IF I HAD FIGURED IT ALL OUT, BUT BEING GROWN, WASN'T IT. I HAD TO REALIZE... THAT MY LIFE WAS JUST GETTING STARTED.

5

Follow My First Instincts

"IGNORING THE SIGNS IS A GOOD WAY TO
END UP IN THE WRONG DESTINATION"-
UNKNOWN

IT WAS A PARTY IN THE NEIGHBORHOOD THIS
GIRL DESI WAS THROWING. KELSEY STARTED
HANGING WITH DESI A LOT. KELSEY CALLED
ME AND TOLD ME TO COME BECAUSE SHE
HADN'T SEEN ME. EVERYBODY WAS GONNA BE
THERE SO I KNEW I NEEDED TO BE THERE AS
WELL. I ENDED UP GOING TO THE PARTY AND
THE WHOLE HOOD WAS THERE. I WAS
DANCING AND EXCHANGING NUMBERS WITH
THIS BOY NAMED JOE. DESI'S BASEMENT WAS
SO PACKED. WE WERE HIP-ROLLING OFF
PRETTY RICKY AND HEEL-TOEING. IT WAS SO
HOT AND PACKED DOWN THERE THAT I HAD
TO GO OUTSIDE FOR SOME AIR. THERE WERE
MORE PEOPLE OUTSIDE. IT WAS THIS BOY
NAMED "TIM" OUT THERE I WAS TALKING TO.
HE WAS COOL AND HE LIKED ME AND I REALLY
WASN'T INTERESTED IN HIM. BUT HE ASKED ME
TO RIDE WITH HIM RIGHT QUICK TO MAKE A
COUPLE OF MOVES AND WE WERE COMING
RIGHT BACK. I REALLY DIDN'T WANT TO
LEAVE BECAUSE THE PARTY WAS BANGING,
BUT I DID WANT TO GO FOR A RIDE. I AGREED
AND SAID, "LET'S GO 'CAUSE I ALREADY GOT A
NUMBER FOR THE NIGHT".

WE RIDIN' HE MAKES A COUPLE STOPS THEN
HE PULLS UP TO A MOTEL OFF 8 MILE. NOW I'M
NOT PAYING ATTENTION TO MY

SURROUNDINGS WHILE HE DRIVES BUT NOW THAT WE STOPPED I'M TRYNA SEE WHAT'S GOING ON. I'M THINKING MAYBE HE IS MEETING SOMEBODY HERE. I'M GETTING A LITTLE CONFUSED ABOUT WHAT'S GOING ON BUT I DON'T SAY ANYTHING. TIM GETS OUT OF THE CAR TO GO TO THE LOBBY. I'M JUST SITTING THERE LOOKING AROUND BUT IN MY HEAD, I'M LIKE "I KNOW HE DOESN'T THINK WE BOUT TO HAVE SEX", AND "I KNOW HE AIN'T MAKE ME LEAVE THE PARTY FOR THIS." HE CAME BACK TO THE CAR AND TOLD ME TO "GET OUT". I'M LIKE "WHY?'' HE LOOKED AT ME AND SAID, "JUST FOR A MINUTE." I'M JUST LOOKING AT HIM SAYING "NO." I SAID "I COULD HAVE STAYED AT THE PARTY" THEN I ASKED HIM, "WHY YOU BRING ME HERE?" HE WAS LIKE "MAN COME ON, STOP PLAYING." SO I GET OUT OF THE CAR AND WE WALK IN THE ROOM, HE LIKE "WE 'BOUT TO CHILL WHILE I WAIT FOR SOMEBODY TO PULL UP." I INSTANTLY GOT NERVOUS. NOW I'M ASKING HIM AGAIN TO JUST TAKE ME BACK TO THE PARTY.

HE WAS LIKE, "GIRL YOU AIN'T GOING NOWHERE JUST CHILL." I AIN'T NERVOUS NO MORE I'M STARTING TO GET MAD. I'M HEATED. I'M ALREADY UNCOMFORTABLE BECAUSE HE BROUGHT ME TO A ROOM. IN MY HEAD I'M

LIKE, "THIS WHAT I GET, ALWAYS HOPPING IN SOMEBODY'S CAR." TIM GETS TO TALKING CRAZY AND TRYING TO RUB UP ON ME. I'M PUSHING HIM OFF TELLING HIM TO STOP TOUCHING ME. HE WAS GETTING MADDER AND MADDER EVERY TIME I PUSHED HIM OFF. SO NOW WE ARE NEARLY ABOUT TO FIGHT BECAUSE HE THINKS HE GOT ME. ONCE HE SEES I'M NOT PLAYING AND STRONG ENOUGH TO DEFEND MYSELF. HE BECAME MAD AND GAVE UP AND TOLD ME TO GET OUT AND FIND MY OWN WAY BACK, 'CAUSE HE WASN'T TAKING ME. I JUST STARTED SNAPPING AND I GOT OUT OF THERE AS FAST AS I COULD. I GOT DOWN TO THE HOTEL LOBBY AND CALLED A CAB.

WHILE I'M WAITING IN THE LOBBY FOR A CAB. I NOTICE TWO GUYS PULL UP IN A CAR WITH TWO WOMEN THEY WALK IN TRYING TO GET A ROOM. AT THIS POINT, I'M STILL IN DISBELIEF FROM WHAT JUST HAPPENED TO ME SO I'M JUST SCARED LOOKING OUT THE WINDOW. PRAYING MY CAB WOULD HURRY UP AND PULL UP AND HOPED THESE GUYS DON'T SAY SOMETHING TO ME. BUT ONE OF THE GUYS JUST HAD TO SAY SOMETHING. HE WAS LIKE, "BABY GIRL, WHAT ARE YOU DOING IN HERE?" I AIN'T SAY NOTHING AT FIRST THEN HE'S LIKE, "WHAT'S WRONG WITH YOU?" "YOU GOT

A MAN ?" "CAN I GET YOUR NUMBER?" I TELL
HIM, "I JUST GOT PUT OUT" AND STARTED
SAYING MY NUMBER OUT LOUD. I JUST
WANTED HIM TO STOP TALKING TO ME. AS I'M
GIVING HIM MY NUMBER THE OTHER GUY
WITH HIM STARTS TAKING MY NUMBER DOWN
TOO. I'M JUST SHAKING MY HEAD THINKING,
"WHERE IS THIS CAB?" THE OTHER GUY ASKED
ME MY NAME AND I TOLD HIM MY FAKE NAME,
KIERA. I ONLY GAVE THEM THE RIGHT
NUMBER JUST IN CASE THEY CALLED ME RIGHT
THERE. I KNEW A GIRL WHO HAD JUST GOT
KILLED FOR NOT GIVING A GUY HER NUMBER.
SO I WASN'T PLAYING THOSE KINDS OF GAMES.
I JUST WANTED THE NIGHT TO BE OVER AT
THIS POINT. BY THE TIME I SAID THE NAME
KIERA OUT OF MY MOUTH THE CAB WAS
PULLING UP. BOTH GUYS WERE LIKE "I'M
GONNA CALL YOU", I DIDN'T CARE WHAT THEY
WERE SAYING I WAS SO HAPPY TO SEE THAT
CAB. I RAN OUT OF THAT LOBBY SO FAST. I
JUST COULDN'T BELIEVE WHAT TIM TRIED TO
PULL. THERE WERE SO MANY RED FLAGS I
IGNORED THAT NIGHT.

6

That One Phone Call

"WE DON'T MEET PEOPLE BY ACCIDENT.
THERE'S ALWAYS A REASON,
A BLESSING OR A LESSON"- DEEPA

A COUPLE OF DAYS GO BY AND I GET A PHONE CALL ASKING TO "SPEAK TO KIERA?" I LOOKED AT THE PHONE AND RESPONDED, "WHO IS THIS, YOU HAVE THE WRONG NUMBER". HE RESPONDED, "NO I DON'T, THIS GHOST, I TOOK YOUR NUMBER DOWN AT THE MOTEL WHILE MY BOY WAS GETTING YOUR NUMBER". I COULDN'T DO NOTHING BUT LAUGH AND SAID "WHAT'S UP?" I COULDN'T BELIEVE HE ACTUALLY CALLED. NOW I WAS INTRIGUED BECAUSE HE CAUGHT ME UP WITH MY FAKE NAME. HE'S LIKE, "WHAT'S UP WITH YOU?" I TOLD HIM "THAT'S CRAZY BECAUSE YOUR BOY NEVER CALLED AND HE WAS THE ONE WHO ASKED ME FOR MY NUMBER". HE LAUGHED. WE TALKED A FEW TIMES, THEN HE FINALLY CAME TO PICK ME UP. I'M A LITTLE NERVOUS BECAUSE I REALLY DON'T REMEMBER HOW HE LOOKS BUT I KNOW HE IS OLDER. WHEN HE PULLED UP I RUSHED TO THE CAR SO CAT WOULDN'T CATCH ME LEAVING. BUT SHE CAUGHT ME. SHE CAME TO THE CAR AND ASKED HIM TWENTY-ONE QUESTIONS BEFORE WE PULLED OFF. SHE DID THAT EVERY TIME I LEFT WITH SOMEONE. THAT WAS A SIGN RIGHT THERE THAT I WAS YOUNG BUT HE IGNORED IT AND WE HUNG OUT. WE HUNG OUT A FEW MORE TIMES UNTIL ONE DAY WE WERE HANGING OUT TRYING TO GO TO THE BAR AND I DIDN'T HAVE AN ID TO GET IN. I EVENTUALLY HAD TO TELL HIM MY AGE. I WAS

SIXTEEN GOING ON SEVENTEEN AT THE TIME.
WHEN I TOLD HIM HE COULDN'T BELIEVE IT.
HE WAS SHOCKED BUT PISSED AT THE SAME
TIME. HE CUT ME OFF FOR A WHILE. I DIDN'T
HEAR FROM HIM FOR WEEKS. THEN FINALLY I
GOT A CALL FROM HIM. I SAID, "I GUESS
YOU'RE NOT MAD ANYMORE". "HE RESPONDED,
"I COULDN'T HELP MYSELF. WE ARE ALREADY
TOO DEEP IN. PLUS YOU DON'T CARRY
YOURSELF LIKE YOU ARE YOUNG." I SHOULD
HAVE BEEN UPFRONT WITH HIM BUT HE NEVER
ASKED SO I NEVER SAID ANYTHING. WE HUNG
OUT ON AND OFF FOR A MINUTE.

IN THE MEANTIME, I FINALLY CALLED JOE, THE
ONE GUY'S NUMBER I GOT AT THE PARTY THAT
NIGHT. HE WAS FROM OUR NEIGHBORHOOD SO
I SAW HIM NUMEROUS TIMES BEFORE. HE WAS
MORE OF A HOMIE THAT TURNED INTO MY
BOYFRIEND. THINGS GOT SERIOUS WITH US.
JOE WAS A COUPLE OF YEARS OLDER THAN ME
I WOULD SAY ABOUT THREE YEARS AND HE
WAS IN THE STREETS MAKING MOVES. HE
MADE SURE I WAS STRAIGHT. RATHER IT WAS
WEED, MONEY, OR FOOD I DIDN'T GO
WITHOUT. MARIE WOULD LET HIM SPEND THE
NIGHT FROM TIME TO TIME. HE MADE SURE
SHE WAS GOOD MANY DAYS AS WELL. JOE
WOULD TAKE ME TO SCHOOL OR HE LET ME
DRIVE HIS CAR TO SCHOOL. HE HAD AN 04

MERCURY MARAUDER WITH A NICE PAINT JOB,
THAT WAS THE HOTTEST CAR BACK THEN. THE
DAYS I DROVE TO SCHOOL YOU COULDN'T
TELL ME ANYTHING. I USED TO PULL UP TO
SCHOOL THINKING I WAS THAT DEAL. ALL MY
FRIENDS WERE ASKING WHERE I GOT THE CAR
FROM.

JOE AND I HAD OUR LITTLE RELATIONSHIP
ISSUES WHERE OUR TRUST WAS FADING. I
WOULD CATCH HIM DOING PLENTY OF
THINGS. SO I WAS STILL DOING ME WHENEVER
I GOT A CHANCE WITH GHOST AND THESE
TWO OTHER GUYS I HAD AS BACKUP. BUT
OTHER THAN THAT WE JUST VIBED AND DID
US. THINGS CHANGED WHEN JOE WENT TO
JAIL. EVERYTHING JUST FELL APART FOR ME.
WHEN HE WENT IN I FOUND OUT I WAS TWO
MONTHS PREGNANT. I DIDN'T TELL HIM AT
FIRST. I DIDN'T WANT TO TELL ANYBODY. I
KNEW I HAD BEEN MESSING AROUND. BUT I
WAS OUT WITH GHOST AND GOT SICK. I
ENDED UP TELLING HIM FIRST. HE ASKED IF IT
WAS HIS. I SAID, "NO." THEN MARIE CAUGHT
ON TO ME CAUSE WHEN I WOULD GET READY
FOR SCHOOL I WOULD BE IN THAT BATHROOM
FOR AN HOUR THROWING UP. SHE ASKED
SEVERAL TIMES "ARE YOU PREGNANT?" I
WOULD LIE AND SAY "NO." ONE TIME I TOLD
HER I HAD A STOMACH VIRUS TRYING TO

HIDE IT. OR I HAD A HANGOVER. I CAME UP
WITH ANY EXCUSE TO THROW HER OFF.
DIDN'T KNOW WHY I WAS AFRAID TO TELL,
WASN'T LIKE SHE WAS A STRICT PARENT. SHE
WAS VERY UNDERSTANDING AND WANTED ME
TO TELL HER IF SOMETHING WAS WRONG. I
JUST WAS ASHAMED AND WASN'T READY. ON
TOP OF THAT, ALL I COULD THINK ABOUT IS
MY AUNT KASH TALKING CRAP TELLING ME I
WAS GOING TO BE A BUM AND NOT GONNA
ACCOMPLISH ANYTHING IN LIFE IF I HAD A
BABY SO THAT WAS STUCK IN MY HEAD. I
DIDN'T WANT TO BE JUDGED BY OTHERS. I
ALSO KNEW I WASN'T READY TO BE A MOM.

7

Cap and Gown Don't Define Me

"I'M ALWAYS BEING TESTED, AND I DON'T
KNOW THE SUBJECT

AND I DON'T HAVE A TEACHER,

BUT I FEEL SO INSTRUCTED"- A$AP ROCKY

SCHOOL WAS ALWAYS A CHALLENGE FOR ME. I GOT KICKED OUT OF EVERY MIDDLE SCHOOL FOR FIGHTING AND JUST FOR MY BEHAVIOR OVERALL. THE SAME ATTITUDE I LEFT MIDDLE SCHOOL WITH I CARRIED OVER INTO HIGH SCHOOL. MOST OF THE TIME I GOT IN TROUBLE FOR FIGHTING AND BEING RUDE TO MY TEACHERS. IN MY FIRST YEAR OF HIGH SCHOOL, I GOT KICKED OUT OF ALL DETROIT PUBLIC SCHOOLS FOR A YEAR. THEN I HAD TO ATTEND AN ALTERNATIVE SCHOOL. ONCE I COMPLETED THAT, THEY SENT ME TO MLK HIGH SCHOOL. THAT WAS A BIG DEAL FOR ME BECAUSE IT WAS A GOOD SCHOOL. IT'S LOCATED ON THE EAST SIDE OF DETROIT SO I WENT TO STAY WITH C-JAY DAD, WHO IS MY GRANDAD SPEEDY. OVER THERE IT WAS A BETTER ENVIRONMENT FOR ME. I SOMEHOW MANAGED TO GO BACK AND FORTH BETWEEN MARIE AND SPEEDY HOUSE. I WOULD GO TO MARIE'S HOUSE 'CAUSE THERE WAS MORE FREEDOM OVER THERE. SPEEDY HAD A LITTLE MORE STRUCTURE IN HIS HOUSE. I MIGHT HAVE BEEN A LITTLE TOO MUCH TO DEAL WITH. SO SPEEDY AND HIS STEPDAUGHTERS BOOTED ME OUT. THEY WERE TIRED OF ME AND REALLY NEEDED TO MAKE SPACE FOR THE CHILDREN THEY WERE ABOUT TO HAVE. SO NOW I WAS BACK WITH MARIE FULLY AND WE WERE STAYING ON THIRD STREET AT THE TIME. I HAD STOPPED GOING TO MLK HIGH

SCHOOL BECAUSE IT WAS TOO FAR FROM THE
HOUSE SO I WAS KICKED OUT DUE TO MY
ATTENDANCE. I HAD TO FIND A SCHOOL
CLOSER TO WHERE WE STAYED. I WAS REALLY
HURT BECAUSE NOW, I WASN'T GONNA BE
WITH MY FRIENDS ANYMORE. IT WAS LIKE
FIFTEEN OF US WE WERE CALLED THE GOON
SQUAD. WE RAN MLK. YOU COULDN'T TELL US
ANYTHING. A LOT OF KIDS WERE SCARED OF
US. WE ALL STUCK TOGETHER FROM THE
FIGHTS, SKIPPING CLASS, AND RUNNING FROM
SARGE, THE HALL SECURITY, CAUSE WE DIDN'T
HAVE A HALL PASS. WE DID IT ALL TOGETHER
AND TOOK WHATEVER CONSEQUENCES CAME
WITH IT TOGETHER. I WAS GOING TO MISS
THEM. THOSE WERE THE GOOD DAYS

 I STARTED GOING TO CROSSMAN
ALTERNATIVE HIGH SCHOOL DURING MY
JUNIOR AND SENIOR YEARS. IN MY SENIOR
YEAR, I COMPLETELY STOPPED GOING. I WAS
TOO SICK TO EVEN SIT IN CLASS ALL DAY.
THERE I WAS PREGNANT AND ALL MY FRIENDS
WERE GETTING READY FOR GRADUATION DAY
AND GOING OFF TO PROM. I WATCHED A
COUPLE OF MY FRIENDS OFF TO PROM. I WAS
HAPPY FOR THEM BUT I FELT LIKE I HAD
FAILED MYSELF.

AT THIS POINT, ALL OF THOSE DECISIONS I
HAD MADE WERE STARTING TO HIT ME THE
CLOSER I CAME TO ACTUALLY BEING GROWN.
LOOKING BACK I REALLY WISH I HAD
SOMEONE TO ADMIRE WHO COULD HAVE TOLD
ME NOT TO QUIT OR SOMEONE IN MY EAR
SAYING "YOU CAN FINISH SCHOOL." BUT I WAS
ALL OVER THE PLACE, LOOKING FOR LOVE
AND ATTENTION IN THE WRONG PLACES.
TRYING TO BE GROWN NOT REALIZING ALL
THE CRAZY STUFF THAT COMES WITH BEING
GROWN. I JUST WISH I WASN'T IN SUCH A
RUSH. I JUST KNEW I WAS GONNA BE ABLE TO
EXPERIENCE A PROM AND WALK ACROSS THAT
STAGE. INSTEAD OF ME EXPERIENCING THOSE
THINGS I WAS GETTING READY TO SKIP SOME
STEPS AND JUMP RIGHT INTO BEING A
MOTHER. RIGHT INTO BEING THE HEAD OF
SOMEONE'S LIFE. BUT IF I KNEW WHAT I KNOW
NOW, I WOULD HAVE FINISHED SCHOOL WITH
A HIGH SCHOOL DIPLOMA. I UNDERSTAND
NOW THE VALUE OF THAT SMALL
ACCOMPLISHMENT OR JUST EVEN
EXPERIENCING THE MOMENT. IT'S NOT SO
MUCH THAT IT'S GONNA STOP ME FROM BEING
SUCCESSFUL. BUT IT WOULD HAVE SHOWN MY
MENTAL STRENGTH TO GO AGAINST WHAT
THOSE AROUND ME HAD ALREADY SAID
ABOUT ME.

MOST OF MY BROTHERS AND SISTERS
GRADUATED FROM HIGH SCHOOL, BUT THEY
ALL HAD A BETTER SUPPORT SYSTEM THAN I
DID. BUT EVEN WITH THAT BEHIND THEM, AT
THIS POINT IN LIFE, I'M DOING BETTER THAN
THEM ALL. AS MUCH AS I WISH I HAD THE
SUPPORT THEY HAD, I DON'T REGRET MY
PATH. SCHOOL IS JUST NOT FOR EVERYONE
AND THE PEOPLE WHO ARE ABLE TO STICK IT
OUT HAVE FOUND A WAY TO GET THROUGH IT.
ALTHOUGH SCHOOL I WOULD SAY DEFINITELY
WASN'T FOR ME BUT IT WOULD HAVE BEEN
BENEFICIAL IN THE LONG RUN. SCHOOL
DEFINITELY DOESN'T DEFINE ME.

8

Most Beautiful Pain

"A WOMAN IN BIRTH IS ALL AT ONCE HER MOST POWERFUL, AND MOST VULNERABLE.

BUT ANY WOMAN WHO HAS BIRTHED UNDERSTANDS THAT WE ARE STRONGER THAN WE KNOW AT THAT MOMENT OF BIRTH AND CARRY THAT STRENGTH AFTER" - MARCIE MACARI

NOW I HAD TO PUT MY BIG GIRL PANTIES ON.
I'M NINETEEN YEARS OLD AND I WAS ABOUT
TO BECOME A MOTHER. I KNEW I HAD
SOMEONE TO PROTECT NOW AND THAT
DEPENDS ON ME. SO I KNEW I HAD TO DO
WHATEVER IT TOOK FOR US TO BE GOOD. I
HAD VERY LITTLE TO NO SUPPORT. I HAD A
LOT TO FIGURE OUT. I WAS JUDGED A LOT
BECAUSE I WAS A YOUNG MOM. C-JAY'S
MOTHER, WHO IS MY GRANDMA MANDY,
REMINDED ME THAT I COULD ALWAYS DEPEND
ON HER IF I NEEDED ANYTHING. SHE LET ME
STAY WITH HER TO PREPARE MYSELF FOR
MOTHERHOOD. SHE EVEN GAVE ME A BABY
SHOWER. SHE MADE SURE I HAD EVERYTHING
TO PREPARE FOR MY BABY TO COME INTO
THIS WORLD.

HERE IT WAS MAY 29, 2010, AND I JUST BOUGHT
THE BEST THING THAT EVER HAPPENED TO ME
IN THE WORLD. THE LOVE OF MY LIFE,
CAMAREE J., ALSO KNOWN AS MAREE. I CAN'T
DESCRIBE THE FEELING BUT I KNOW IT FELT
GOOD. MY BUTTERCUP WAS FINALLY HERE AND
I STILL DIDN'T HAVE IT ALL TOGETHER. BUT
THAT DIDN'T MATTER AT THE MOMENT. WHAT
MATTERED WAS THIS NEW LIFE. WHAT
MATTERED WAS THIS NEW MOTIVATION I HAD
TO PUSH FORWARD. NO MATTER WHAT MY LIFE

HAD LOOKED LIKE BEFORE THIS MOMENT IT
DIDN'T REALLY MATTER. I WAS A PARENT TO A
WHOLE HUMAN. BEING A MOM TOOK A LOT
MORE FROM ME THAN ANYTHING I HAD GIVEN
MY ENERGY TO AT THIS POINT. MEANWHILE,
MY NOW EX-BOYFRIEND JOE, WHO WAS
SUPPOSED TO BE THE FATHER, WAS GONE FOR
10 YEARS. THEN I TOLD GHOST NOT TO WORRY
AND THAT THE BABY WASN'T HIS. BUT HE WAS
SECOND-GUESSING ME. NOW MY NEW
BOYFRIEND LOUIS, STOOD BY ME AND HELPED
ME DURING MY WHOLE PREGNANCY. EVERY
STEP OF THE WAY WITH MY BABY HE WAS
RIGHT THERE. BUT DEEP DOWN INSIDE I KNEW
LOUIS WASN'T THE FATHER AND I KNEW IT
WASN'T RIGHT TO MAKE HIM THINK THAT HE
WAS. BUT I ALSO KNEW I COULDN'T DO IT
ALONE. NOW ALTHOUGH MY CHILD WAS A
BLESSING AND I WAS TRYING TO FIGURE
MYSELF OUT AT THE SAME TIME BEING A
YOUNG MOM, THE OTHER STUFF THAT CAME
ALONG WITH MOTHERHOOD I DON'T THINK I
WAS PREPARED FOR. NOW, I PLAYED A PART IN
THE WAY THINGS WENT BUT A LOT OF STUFF
WAS VERY UNNECESSARY AS WELL.

I HADN'T SEEN GHOST SINCE I TOLD HIM I
WAS PREGNANT AND THE BABY WASN'T HIS.
HE WOULD CALL TO CHECK ON ME. BUT THEN
HE POPS UP ASKING IF HE CAN SEE THE BABY

NOW THAT MAREE IS BORN. I WAS HESITANT AT FIRST. BUT I LET HIM COME SEE THE BABY BECAUSE HE KEPT ASKING. WHEN HE SAW MAREE HE SAID "YOU SURE THIS AIN'T MY BABY? HE LOOKS LIKE US, WILLIS." I'M STILL SAYING, "NAW MAN THIS AIN'T YOU, GONE ON." BUT AT THE SAME TIME, I WAS SECOND-GUESSING MYSELF NOW BECAUSE I'M TRYING TO FIGURE OUT WHERE MAREE GOT THIS LITTLE FAT NOSE FROM. I REALLY DIDN'T WANT HIM TO BE THE FATHER BECAUSE ALL I KNEW ABOUT GHOST WAS A GOOD TIME. I DIDN'T KNOW WHAT TYPE OF FATHER HE WOULD BE. AFTER THAT VISIT, HE GOT GHOST JUST LIKE HIS NAME AND HE DISAPPEARED FOR A WHILE.

NOW JOE IS STARTING TO ASK TO SEE THE BABY AND FOR ME TO SEND HIM PICTURES. JOE SENT HIS MOM OVER TO COME TO SEE MY BABY. SHE COMES AND SAYS "OH YOU HAVE EVERYTHING FOR YOUR BABY AND HE LOOKS LIKE MY OTHER GRANDKIDS." IN MY HEAD, I'M LIKE "NO HE DOESN'T." MY BABY GOT HIS OWN LITTLE LOOK WITH THIS FAT NOSE. AFTER SHE LEFT I WROTE JOE A LETTER AND I TOLD JOE "MAREE MIGHT NOT BE YOURS ." HE WROTE BACK, "LET'S GET A BLOOD TEST." I TOLD HIM IT WOULD BE A PROCESS BECAUSE HE IS IN JAIL SO I'M JUST GOING TO TEST THE OTHER

GUY AND WE WOULD TAKE IT FROM THERE.
THE OTHER GUY WAS GHOST BUT HE WAS IN
AND OUT. SO I HAD TO COME UP WITH A WAY
TO TELL GHOST I NEEDED A BLOOD TEST. I
JUST DIDN'T SEE HIM BEING THE FATHER,
ESPECIALLY AFTER I ALREADY TOLD HIM HE
WASN'T THE FATHER. I MESSED UP BIG TIME. I
PUSHED GHOST AWAY SO MANY TIMES BUT
NOW I NEEDED HIM. I DIDN'T REALLY CARE IF
HE WAS THE FATHER OR NOT BECAUSE I HAD
LOUIS THAT WASN'T MISSING A BEAT.

9

I owe myself an apology

"THERE ARE APOLOGIES I'M STILL OWED AND APOLOGIES THAT WILL PROBABLY NEVER COME, BUT BY FAR THE MOST IMPORTANT APOLOGIES ARE THE ONES I OWE MYSELF.

FOR NOT THINKING I WAS ENOUGH,

FOR NOT THINKING I WAS WORTHY,

FOR NOT REALIZING MY MAGIC BEFORE"-BILLY CHAPATA

LOUIS WAS EVERYTHING A CHILD NEEDED IN A FATHER. LOUIS ALWAYS KEPT MY POCKETS FULL AND MY STOMACH FED. HE GOT ME MY FIRST FOREIGN CAR, A 2012 INFINITI G-35X. IT WAS A CHAMPAGNE COLOR. I WAS TOO YOUNG AND DIDN'T REALIZE WHAT I HAD. HE CARED SO MUCH ABOUT ME, HE GOT MAREE AND ME A HOUSE. HE MOVED IN AND THAT'S WHEN I REALLY GOT TO SEE HIS TRUE COLORS. EVERYTHING STARTED GOING DOWNHILL WITH US. IT WAS A NO-DEAL FOR ME. ONCE HE GOT US ALL SETTLED IN THE HOUSE HE WANTED TO BE IN CONTROL OF EVERYTHING! SAYING WHAT I CAN AND CAN'T DO. LISTEN, HADN'T ANY MAN TOLD ME WHAT I WAS OR WASN'T GONNA DO BEFORE AND IT FOR DAMN SURE WASN'T ABOUT TO START NOW. I APPRECIATED THE STABILITY BUT NOT AT THE EXPENSE OF MY FREEDOM. I HAD TO GET AWAY BEFORE THINGS GOT WORSE. THAT'S WHEN I KNEW I WANTED MY OWN AND NOT A HANDOUT. ONCE I CAME TO THAT UNDERSTANDING WITH MYSELF I KNEW I HAD TO GET IT ON MY OWN. WHEN I SAY I WENT AND GOT IT ON MY OWN I DON'T MEAN I JUST JUMPED UP AND WENT AND GOT A JOB. NAH I GOT UP AND JUMPED IN MY BAG. I JUMPED IN MY SELF-IMPROVEMENT BAG, I JUMPED IN MY THIS IS FOR MY FUTURE BAG. I HAD SO MANY

THINGS TO PROVE BUT MORE IMPORTANTLY, I
HAD TO PROVE TO MYSELF THAT I WAS AS LIT
AS I KNEW I WAS. THAT MEANT GOING TO
KNOCK OUT SOME OF THE SMALLER GOALS I
HAD LEFT UNDONE. FOR STARTERS, I GOT UP
OFF THAT COUCH AND WENT TO EVEREST
INSTITUTE WHERE I GOT MY GED AND BECAME
A MEDICAL ADMINISTRATIVE ASSISTANT.
AFTER I GRADUATED, I GOT MY VERY FIRST
JOB AT MEDICAL ONE FOOT DOCTOR IN TROY.
I FINALLY WAS ON THE RIGHT TRACK TO
ACCOMPLISHING THINGS.

EVEN THOUGH I MADE TEN STEPS TO GET
AHEAD I WAS STILL BACK AT SQUARE ONE
STAYING WITH MARIE WITH A BABY. I HAD
LEFT LOUIS AND I STILL WASN'T MAKING
ENOUGH TO GET MY OWN PLACE. THINGS
STILL DIDN'T FEEL GOOD ENOUGH. I WAS FED
UP WITH STAYING WITH MARIE. SO I WENT
RIDING LOOKING AT VACANT HOUSES THAT
STILL HAD A ROOF, WINDOWS, AND A GAS
METER. AS LONG AS IT WAS LIVEABLE I WENT
IN, CHANGED THE LOCKS, AND SQUATTED AS
LONG AS I COULD. ME AND MAREE THUGGED
IT OUT BUT LOUIS STILL HELPED WITH MAREE.
HE WOULD KEEP MAREE WHENEVER I ASKED SO
MAREE DIDN'T EXPERIENCE TOO MUCH OF THE
WASHING UP IN COLD WATER OR EVEN THE
COLD NIGHTS WITH FIVE HEATERS PLUGGED

UP AT ONCE. I DID WHAT I HAD TO DO TO
MAKE THINGS HAPPEN ON MY OWN.

NOW MAREE IS FOUR GOING ON FIVE AND ALL
HE KNOWS IS LOUIS BECAUSE THAT'S WHO
WAS THERE FROM DAY ONE WITH HIM. GHOST
MADE SURE HE STAYED IN CONTACT. HE
STARTED COMING AROUND MORE AND MORE.
WE WERE BACK TO OUR HANGING DAYS.
EVERYBODY NOTICED MAREE AND GHOST
LOOKED LIKE TWINS. I STILL DIDN'T SEE IT. I
WAS STILL SAYING MY BABY LOOKED LIKE
HIMSELF. I WAS ALSO EAGER TO FIND OUT
WHETHER GHOST WAS REALLY HIS DAD AT
THAT POINT. SO NOW IS THE TIME TO ASK HIM
TO TAKE THE TEST. SO I JUST TELL HIM, "I
THINK WE SHOULD TAKE A BLOOD TEST SINCE
YOU KEEP SECOND-GUESSING ME." HE AGREED
TO TAKE IT. HE TOLD ME TO LET HIM KNOW
WHEN I FIND A PLACE AND SET UP AN
APPOINTMENT. NOW MADDIE AND I ARE
MAKING BETS ON THE BLOOD TEST. SHE GOT
HER MONEY ON GHOST AND MINES WAS ON
JOE. $100 BET !! FOR SOME REASON, I JUST
DIDN'T WANT GHOST TO BE HIS FATHER. THE
DAY FINALLY CAME, WE TOOK THE TEST AND
THE RESULTS WERE IN. THE MAN CALLED
WITH THE RESULTS, MY HEART WAS BEATING
FAST. THE MAN SAID MS. ADAMS GHOST IS

99.99 PERCENT THE FATHER. I JUST PAUSED
AND SAID THANK YOU. AS I'M HANGING UP
GHOST CALLS ME I ANSWER AND WE BOTH
JUST HELD THE PHONE IN SILENCE. THEN
AFTER A MINUTE, WE BURST OUT LAUGHING.
GHOST SAID, "MAN, I FELT IT I KNEW HE WAS
MINE." HE WAS MAD BECAUSE I HAD PUSHED
HIM AWAY. NOW MAREE ALREADY GREW A
BOND WITH LOUIS. I WAS GUILTY AND
EMBARRASSED. I LEGIT DIDN'T WANT HIM TO
BE THE FATHER. I ALSO FELT RELIEVED AND
HAPPY FOR MY BABY. I STILL OWE MADDIE
UNTIL THIS DAY FOR THAT BET.

NOW I HAD TO BREAK THE NEWS TO LOUIS. I
TOLD HIM THE RESULTS OF THE DNA TEST,
AND HIS EXACT WORDS WERE, "SO, THAT
AIN'T CHANGING NOTHING. I'M STILL GOING
TO BE THERE FOR HIM". THAT WAS THE
REALEST THING I HEARD ALL MY LIFE. SO NOW
I HAD SOME EXPLAINING TO DO TO MAREE. I
TOLD HIM WHAT WAS GOING ON. MOST
IMPORTANTLY I DIDN'T WANT MY BABY
CONFUSED, HURT, OR QUESTIONED WHEN HE
GOT OLDER SO I FELT LIKE THE BEST THING
FOR ME TO DO WAS TO COME CLEAN AND LET
HIM KNOW WHILE HE WAS STILL YOUNG.
BECAUSE THIS SITUATION WASN'T HURTING
ME. IT WAS ONLY GOING TO AFFECT MAREE IN
THE LONG RUN. HE WAS A LITTLE CONFUSED

BUT HE CAUGHT ON. THANKFULLY LOUIS WAS
A MAN OF HIS WORD. THAT TEST REALLY
DIDN'T CHANGE ANYTHING. HE WAS THERE
FOR MAREE AND GHOST WAS STILL IN AND
OUT. GHOST'S EXCUSE FOR EVERYTHING WAS
THAT IT WAS GONNA BE HARD TO BREAK THE
BOND BETWEEN MAREE AND LOUIS, BECAUSE
THAT WAS ALL MAREE WAS USED TO. I
EVENTUALLY STOPPED WORRYING ABOUT
GHOST AND LET GOD HANDLE HIM. I NEVER
ASKED GHOST FOR ANYTHING, BUT HE HAS
BEEN THERE FOR MAREE'S MOST IMPORTANT
DAYS OR SPECIAL DAYS. HE'S STEPPED UP
MORE AS FAR AS SPENDING TIME-WISE. AS FOR
LOUIS, HE IS THE REAL DEFINITION OF A
"REAL FATHER." HE SUPPORTS MAREE WITH
EVERYTHING. HE HAS BEEN THERE MENTALLY,
FINANCIALLY, AND PHYSICALLY THROUGH IT
ALL. MAREE GOT LUCKY. MAREE IS SUPER
BLESSED TO HAVE TWO FATHERS. HE LOVES
THEM BOTH AND TREATS THEM THE SAME.
MAREE IS THE LIGHT BETWEEN US THREE. HE
IS THE GOOD THAT ALL OF US HAVE IN
COMMON. BUT ANYTHING OTHER THAN HIM
WAS JUST PLAIN O' TOXIC. LOUIS WANTED TO
BE IN CONTROL AND WE NEVER SEEM TO SEE
EYE TO EYE, AND GHOST WAS JUST A WHOLE
OTHER SITUATION.

IO

Living Through The Pain

ON THE COUNT OF 3

EVERYBODY YELL FREE GOOSE!

#MYBROTHERSKEEPER

IN THE MIDST OF ME TRYING TO GET MY LIFE TOGETHER OF COURSE LIFE DOESN'T STOP. LIFE DOESN'T STOP THROWING THINGS AT YOU JUST BECAUSE YOU HAVE STARTED TO FIGURE OUT THE MESS YOU ALREADY HAVE ON YOUR PLATE. SUPPORT IS RARE. SUPPORT FROM A FAMILY WHO ARE ALL IN THE SAME PLACE OF TRYNA FIGURE STUFF OUT IS EVEN RARER. BUT IT'S ALWAYS A FEW IN THE FAMILY THAT NO MATTER WHAT THEY ARE GOING THROUGH ARE GOING TO TRY THEIR HARDEST TO BE THERE FOR PEOPLE. MY BROTHER GOOSE WAS ONE OF THOSE PEOPLE FOR ME. HE WAS MY FOURTH SIBLING FROM MARIE. IF WE ARE BEING HONEST HE IS MY FAVORITE SIBLING. GOOSE WAS A MAN LONG BEFORE HE BECAME A MAN. MEANING HE WAS DEPENDABLE. HE KNEW TO TAKE CARE OF HIS SISTERS AND DID WHAT HE HAD TO DO. HE WOULD MAKE SURE I WAS STRAIGHT EVERY CHANCE HE GOT. HE DID STUFF LIKE PUT GAS IN MY CAR AND KEPT MONEY IN MY POCKETS. HE EVEN BROUGHT ME MY FIRST DESIGNER BAG. I KNEW FOR A FACT HE COULDN'T AFFORD IT CAUSE I COULDN'T. BUT I DIDN'T ASK WHERE HE GOT IT FROM. I HONESTLY DIDN'T CARE. WHETHER IT WAS MONEY OR GIFTS I WAS JUST HAPPY TO HAVE IT. HE WOULD CALL ME EVERY TIME HE NEEDED SOMETHING AND I WOULD DO THE SAME WITH

HIM. I HAD HIS FRONT AND HE DEFINITELY
HAD MY BACK.

IT WAS NOW 2012 AND OUR BOND WAS NOW
BROKEN APART. I GOT A CALL SAYING TO
COME TO THE HOSPITAL GOOSE HAD BEEN
SHOT IN THE FACE AND ARM. WHEN I ARRIVED
I WAS A NERVOUS WRECK. THEY WOULDN'T
LET ME GO BACK TO SEE HIM, ONLY MARIE
COULD BE BACK THERE. I'M ASKING WHAT
HAPPENED AND TRYING TO GET ANSWERS
FROM HIS HOMEBOYS. NOBODY COULD GIVE
ME AN ANSWER. COME TO FIND OUT GOOSE
WAS ACCUSED OF HAVING A SHOOTOUT WITH
THE POLICE. THIS ACCUSATION LED HIM TO
GET HANDCUFFED TO THE HOSPITAL BED.
IMMEDIATELY AFTER HE WAS OUT OF SURGERY
THEY SHIPPED HIM STRAIGHT OFF TO PRISON.
I NEVER GOT TO SEE HIM OR EVEN KNOW IF HE
HEALED CORRECTLY. GOOSE NOW WOULD END
UP SPENDING HALF HIS LIFE BEHIND BARS AND
THAT WAS A HARD PILL FOR ME TO SWALLOW.
A PIECE OF ME WAS GONE AND I COULDN'T
ACCEPT IT. EVEN THOUGH HE IS ONE PHONE
CALL AWAY, THAT'S JUST NOT ENOUGH. THAT
PHONE LINE IS A ONE-WAY STREET. I HAVE TO
WAIT TO HEAR FROM HIM. AIN'T NO CALLING
IF I NEED SOMETHING OR IF I JUST WANTED
TO HEAR HIS VOICE. I DIDN'T HAVE MY LIFE
TOGETHER TO GO SEE HIM OR EVEN ENOUGH

MONEY TO GET HIM A LAWYER. OVER THE
YEARS THAT EATS ME UP. TO THIS DAY IT
STILL BOTHERS ME. I COULDN'T HELP HIM BUT
I KNOW IT'S A LIGHT AT THE END OF THE
TUNNEL AND EVENTUALLY, I WILL BE ABLE TO
REUNITE WITH MY FAVORITE SIBLING AGAIN. I
JUST HAVE TO HOLD ON UNTIL IT'S HIS TIME.
FREE GOOSE.

 THERE'S NOTHING LIKE A SISTER AND
BROTHER BOND. I LOVE YALL WITH EVERY
BREATH IN ME. NOW THERE IS ONLY ONE STILL
STANDING AND FREE, THE BABY OF THE
BUNCH MOOP, I SEE YOU FOLLOWING YOUR
BIG BROTHER'S FOOTSTEPS. BUT I PRAY YOU
CHOOSE TO TAKE ANOTHER ROUTE AND
KNOW THAT IT IS NEVER TOO LATE.

II

Toxicity x2

SIRI PLAY KENDRICK LAMAR- WE CRY
TOGETHER

"I HELD YOU DOWN"

"YOU JUST KEPT ME DOWN, THAT'S A BIG
DIFFERENCE

STRESSIN' MYSELF TRYNA FIGURE OUT WHY
I'M NOT GOOD ENOUGH

GOING TO CHURCH PRAYING FOR YOU,
SEARCHIN' FOR GOOD IN US"- KENDRICK
LAMAR

NOW, THIS IS WHERE MY LIFE GETS A LITTLE
MORE TOXIC. WHEN WE WERE STILL STAYING
ON THE THIRD STREET WHILE I WAS MESSING
AROUND WITH JOE. MARIE AT THIS TIME HAD
ALSO MET THIS GUY NAMED SANTANA AND
HIS BOYS. SHE INVITED HIM AND HIS BOYS
OVER TO HANG OUT, SMOKE AND PARTY.
WHILE THEY WERE OVER, SANTANA JUST KEPT
STARING AT ME AND GIVING ME THE EYE. SO I
WALK UP TO HIM LIKE, "WHAT'S UP? WHY DO
YOU KEEP STARING?" HE SMILED AND SLID ME
HIS NUMBER. I NEVER CALLED HIM. NOW HE IS
RIDING UP AND DOWN OUR STREET EVERY DAY
IN A 97 PEARL WHITE BOX CAPRICE. SO ONE
DAY I'M BORED HANGING OUT WITH MY HOME
GIRLS AND HAD NOTHING TO DO. I FINALLY
CALLED HIM UP. HE TELLS ME TO PULL UP. MY
GIRLS AND I PULL UP ON HIM. SANTANA ASKS
WHAT WE ARE DRINKING. HE GOES TO THE
LIQUOR STORE TO BUY US A BOTTLE. IT'S
HELLA GUYS OVER THERE. THEY WERE
GAMBLING, DRINKING, AND PARTYING. I
STAYED FOR A MINUTE JUST ENOUGH TO
SMOKE AND GET A BOTTLE AND GET A LITTLE
BUZZ THEN I WOULD DIP. THAT WAS PRETTY
MUCH OUR RELATIONSHIP FOR A WHILE.

WITH SANTANA, IT WAS ALWAYS AN
ON-AND-OFF THING FOR SOME REASON. HE

ALWAYS FOUND ME OR SAW ME OUT IN PUBLIC
SOMEWHERE. HE WAS COOL TO MESS AROUND
WITH BUT I JUST DIDN'T SEE MYSELF BEING IN
A RELATIONSHIP WITH HIM. ALL THAT
CHANGED BECAUSE IT'S NOW 2015 AND I
FINALLY DECIDED TO START TAKING SANTANA
SERIOUSLY. THIS WAS MY SOLUTION TO
TRYING TO GET OVER GHOST 'CAUSE ME AND
GHOST WERE GOING AT IT STRONG. SANTANA
STARTED SHOWING ME ANOTHER SIDE OF HIM.
HE WAS TAKING ME ON DATES. BUYING ME
WHATEVER, HE JUST WAS EVERYTHING I
WANTED GHOST TO BE. SANTANA WAS TAKING
ALL MY TIME AND ATTENTION AT THE TIME.
GHOST DIDN'T LIKE THAT. GHOST WOULD POP
UP AT MY HOUSE. HE EVEN CHASED SANTANA
OUT OF MY HOUSE ONE DAY. THAT STILL
DIDN'T RUN SANTANA AWAY OR CHANGE THE
FACT HE WANTED ME. AFTER ALL THAT,
SANTANA AND I DECIDED TO MAKE IT
OFFICIAL. I MOVED OUT OF MY PLACE AND
SANTANA AND I GOT A PLACE TOGETHER IN
HARPER WOODS. IT WAS A NICE
NEIGHBORHOOD AT THE TIME. SANTANA HAD
THREE BOYS BUT ONLY KEPT THE SECOND
OLDEST BOY WITH HIM ALL THE TIME BECAUSE
THE BOY'S MOTHER WASN'T AROUND, AND I
JUST HAD MAREE. SO THAT WAS COOL WITH
ME. I LIKED HIS SONS, AND THEY LIKED ME.
SANTANA WOULD HUSTLE AND I WOULD
PUNCH THE CLOCK. TO MAKE ENDS MEET. HE

HELPED ME THROUGH MY FIRST NURSING PROGRAM. EVERYTHING WAS GOING GREAT FOR US. BUT THERE WERE DAYS I WOULD GET TIRED OF SANTANA WANTING HIS HOME BOYS AND EVERYBODY TO ALWAYS COME OVER OR SPEND THE NIGHT. PLUS I'M REALLY GETTING TO KNOW HIS SON AND BOY WAS HE SOMETHING DIFFERENT, THAT'S ALL I'M GOING TO SAY. WHEN WE WERE JUST KICKING IT, IT WAS COOL. ALSO WHEN HIS HOMEBOYS WERE GAMBLING WE WOULD CHILL TOGETHER SO IT WASN'T A PROBLEM. BUT NOW IT WAS DIFFERENT. WE WERE BUILDING SOMETHING. WE WERE LAYING A FOUNDATION TO REALLY BE TOGETHER AND I DIDN'T KNOW HIS HOME BOYS WERE A PART OF THAT PACKAGE. ON TOP OF ALL THAT SANTANA WAS A COMPLETE MAMA'S BOY AND I HATED THAT FOR HIM. HE DIDN'T UNDERSTAND WHERE I WAS COMING FROM BECAUSE HE WAS USED TO LIVING LIKE THAT.

IT ALL BEGAN TO GET REALLY FRUSTRATING FOR ME AND WHEN THAT HAPPENED OF COURSE I STARTED LOOKING FOR COMFORT IN FAMILIAR AREAS. I WAS MISSING MY BAD HABIT AGAIN, GHOST. PLUS GHOST HAD BEEN CALLING ME ASKING TO TALK OVER DINNER. I WAS SCARED TO GO BECAUSE I HAD BEEN REJECTING HIM WHENEVER HE CALLED. I ALSO

WAS IN A HAPPY SPACE WITH SANTANA
OVERALL BUT THIS PARTICULAR DAY I WAS
OVER IT AND WANTED TO GET OUT OF THE
HOUSE. SO I AGREED TO MEET UP WITH
GHOST. WHILE WE WERE OUT EATING AND
DRINKING, LAUGHING AND GIGGLING ONE OF
SANTANA'S COUSINS SAW US, TOOK A
PICTURE, AND SENT IT TO SANTANA. I GUESS I
HAD TOO MANY DRINKS TO PEEP WHO IT WAS.
THEY FOR SURE SAW ME BUT I DIDN'T SEE
THEM. MY ATTENTION WAS JUST SO FOCUSED
ON GHOST. GHOST AND I LAUGHED THE
REMAINDER OF THE DATE REKINDLING AND
HAVING A GOOD TIME. WE DIDN'T REALIZE IT
WAS TIME TO GO HOME. WHEN I GOT HOME,
OUR HOUSE WASN'T HOME ANYMORE.
SANTANA HAD FUCKED THE HOUSE UP! HE
RIPPED PICTURES UP AND EVERYTHING. IT
WAS A CLEAR HOUSE. SANTANA AND I WENT
DOWNHILL FROM THERE. THE FIGHTING AND
ARGUING BEGAN AND THE TRUST WAS GONE.
THINGS JUST WEREN'T GOING RIGHT FOR US.
HE STARTED GOING TO SEE FEMALES IN MY
CAR WHILE I WAS AT WORK. ALL TYPES OF
STUFF JUST TO GET BACK AT ME. HE TURNED
HIS GRIND UP A NOTCH. IT CAUGHT UP WITH
HIM, WHICH PUT HIM BEHIND BARS FOR
MONTHS. WE LOST OUR HOUSE AND MOVED IN
WITH HIS MOM. THAT WAS THE WRONG MOVE
FOR ME. I DIDN'T WANT TO STAY THERE. I WAS
JUST UNCOMFORTABLE. AND I DIDN'T HAVE

MAREE AS MUCH. I JUST DIDN'T FEEL LIKE
MYSELF. ONCE SANTANA GOT OUT WE TRIED
TO MAKE OUR RELATIONSHIP WORK. BUT WE
JUST COULDN'T GET RIGHT. I WANTED OUR
RELATIONSHIP TO WORK. IT HAD BEEN THREE
YEARS OF DISHONESTY, PAIN, HURT, AND
ABUSE. FOR SOME REASON, I KEPT TAKING HIM
BACK TRYING TO MAKE THINGS RIGHT. THE
ONLY THING THAT WAS DOING WAS TAKING A
TOLL ON ME.

12

Damaged Love

"IF YOU LOOK INTO YOUR HEART,

WITH A POSITIVE MIND,

TAKE SOME-INVENTORY, OF YOUR WOMAN
AND YOUR GLORY

LEAVE THE BAD THINGS BEHIND.

EVERYBODY'S GOT A STORY, ABOUT LOVE AND
THE GOOD THINGS

BUT FOR THE SPICES OF YOUR LIFE, YOU'VE
GOT TO PAY THE PRICE...IF YOU KNOW WHAT
I MEAN.."- ARETHA FRANKLIN

WE ENDED UP MOVING TO TENNESSEE THINKING US GETTING AWAY AND STARTING FRESH WOULD HELP BUT IT DIDN'T. THE FIGHTING AND ARGUING GOT WORSE. I JUST FELT ALL ALONE BECAUSE HE WAS WITH HIS FAMILY DOWN THERE AND I DIDN'T HAVE A SOUL IN THAT STATE I COULD CALL ON. I WAS TRYING TO GET ON MY FEET AND FINALLY GOT A JOB DOWN THERE BUT SANTANA JUST RAN ME AWAY.

I PACKED ME AND MAREE'S BAGS UP AND MADE SANTANA'S BROTHER'S GIRLFRIEND DROP US OFF AT THE BUS STATION. WE HAD SNACKS BUT I ONLY HAD ENOUGH MONEY TO GET ONE TICKET. I HAD NOBODY TO CALL BACK HOME TO SEND ME SOME MONEY. MAREE AND I SAT THERE ALL DAY. I HAD A LONG TIME TO SIT THERE AND THINK. SANTANA NEVER CALLED TO SEE WHERE I WAS AT. AS WE SAT THERE I MET THIS OLDER MAN AND WE ENDED UP TALKING FOR HOURS. I TOLD HIM WHAT I WAS GOING THROUGH. THE MAN ENDS UP PAYING FOR OUR BUS TICKETS AND GIVING ME EXTRA MONEY TO GET FOOD. BOY WAS THAT A BLESSING BECAUSE I HAD NOTHING FIGURED OUT. WE FINALLY MADE IT TO DETROIT AFTER THAT TWELVE-HOUR DRIVE. I DROPPED MAREE OFF AT LOUIS'S SO I COULD FIGURE OUT OUR LIVING ARRANGEMENTS. LOUIS LOOKED AT ME

AND SAID, "YOU LOOK BLOATED, ARE YOU PREGNANT?" I'M LIKE HELL NAW I BETTER NOT BE. I DIDN'T FEEL OR NOTICE A SIGN OF PREGNANCY. WITH THE LITTLE MONEY I DID HAVE LEFT OVER, I WENT AND BOUGHT A PREGNANCY TEST. I TOOK THE TEST AND THERE I WAS PREGNANT. LOOKING STUPID. I WAS STEAMING AND THERE WAS NOTHING I COULD DO ABOUT IT. I DIDN'T HAVE A POT TO PISS IN AND IT WAS THE WEEK BEFORE CHRISTMAS. IT WAS EITHER MAREE CHRISTMAS OR ABORTION. I FINALLY TALKED TO SANTANA AND TOLD HIM I WAS PREGNANT AND HE WAS THE HAPPIEST MAN IN THE WORLD. MEANWHILE, I WANTED AN ABORTION. I FELT LIKE OUR DRAMA WAS TOO MUCH. I KNEW A BABY WASN'T A GREAT MOVE FOR US AT THE TIME. HE WANTED THE BABY. HE SAID, "I'LL TAKE CARE OF MY BABY." I WAS STUCK WITH THE STALE FACE. AFTER THAT, IT WAS LIKE ALL OUR PROBLEMS WENT OUT THE WINDOW. HE MOVED BACK TO DETROIT. I GOT A JOB, GOT US A HOUSE, AND PREPARED MYSELF TO WELCOME MY SECOND BABY BOY. I DIDN'T HAVE A BABY SHOWER BECAUSE I FELT THAT WOULD'VE BEEN GREEDY TO HAVE ONE A SECOND TIME AROUND AND IT WAS ANOTHER BOY. PLUS HIS FAMILY DIDN'T CARE FOR ME AND MY FAMILY FOR SURE HATED HIM. SO SANTANA WENT OUT AND BROUGHT EVERYTHING A BABY COULD NEED. HE WAS

MORE EXCITED THAN ME. HE ACTED LIKE THIS
WAS HIS FIRST TIME HAVING A CHILD. HE
TOLD ME HE FELT DIFFERENT THIS TIME
BECAUSE HE WAS ACTUALLY WITH ME AND
WATCHED HIS BABY GROW IN THE WOMB AND
HE DIDN'T EXPERIENCE THAT WITH HIS OTHER
CHILDREN. BUT I WAS OVER THE WHOLE
PREGNANCY ONCE I SAW THE ULTRASOUND
AND MY BABY HAD SANTANA'S WHOLE FACE. I
JUST WANTED MY BODY BACK TO NORMAL.

NOW IT WAS TIME TO WELCOME MY SECOND
BIGGEST BLESSING JR. TO THE WORLD. I GOT
THAT SAME FEELING I HAD WITH MY
FIRSTBORN ALL OVER AGAIN. I WAS HAPPY
AND COMPLETE. AS FOR SANTANA HE WAS
EXCITED AND HELPED ME WITH THE BABY FOR
THE MOMENT, BUT THE FIGHTING AND
ARGUING WERE BACK. SANTANA FOOLED ME,
HE HAD DONE A WHOLE 360 AFTER I HAD THE
BABY. IT WAS LIKE HE WAS PLANNING TO GET
BACK AT ME. HE REALLY HAD ME WHERE HE
WANTED ME. THE TABLES TURNED. HE
STARTED STAYING OUT LATE. I CAUGHT HIM
CHEATING NUMEROUS TIMES WITH THE SAME
WOMAN. I WASN'T HAVING IT SO I TRACKED
HIS LOCATION DOWN. I PACKED ME AND JR.
UP AND PULLED UP TO THE WOMAN'S HOUSE
WHERE THE LOCATION HAD SENT ME.
KNOCKED ON THE DOOR. SHE ANSWERED AND

SHUT THE DOOR IN MY FACE AND HE
WOULDN'T COME OUTSIDE. SO I STARTED
BUSTING ALL HIS CAR WINDOWS OUT AND
HERS. AND WENT BACK HOME. SOMEHOW SHE
KNEW WHERE WE WERE STAYING AND CAME
AND BUSTED MY HOUSE WINDOWS OUT.
KARMA HIT ME FAST. I WAS SO FED UP WITH
THE LIES AND CHEATING WITH SANTANA. IT
FELT LIKE IT WAS NEVER GONNA STOP. HE WAS
NEVER ACCOUNTABLE FOR WHAT HE WAS
DOING. EVERY TIME WE WOULD GET INTO IT
HE WOULD BRING GHOST UP. ONE DAY WE
WERE ARGUING IN THE CAR. I JUST WENT
BALLISTIC ON HIM. SANTANA STOPPED THE
CAR. HE GOT OUT OF THE CAR AND TOOK HIS
KEYS AND RAN. SO I SAT THERE AND FOUND A
BROWN PAPER BAG AND LIT IT WITH A
CIGARETTE LIGHTER. I GOT OUT AND THE CAR
WAS IN FLAMES WITHIN THREE MINUTES AND
EXPLODED WITHIN FIVE MINUTES. I COULDN'T
BELIEVE HOW FAST THE FIRE HAD SPREAD BUT
IT WAS TOO LATE TO TRY TO PUT THE FIRE
OUT. PEOPLE WERE IN THE WINDOWS
LOOKING. I STARTED HEARING FIRE TRUCKS. I
TOOK OFF SO FAST. I RAN AS FAR AS I COULD
AND CALLED MADDIE TO COME TO GET ME. I
WAS HIDDEN FOUR BLOCKS OVER BEHIND
SOMEBODY'S HOUSE BY THE TIME SHE
ARRIVED. I DON'T KNOW WHAT TOOK OVER
ME BECAUSE I WAS COMPLETELY SOBER. BUT I
NEVER WANT TO BE IN THAT MENTAL STATE

AGAIN. SANTANA'S FAMILY HATES ME EVEN
MORE FOR THAT. THEY THINK I'M JUST THIS
BAD PERSON. BUT NOBODY CARED ABOUT
WHAT LED ME TO THAT SPACE. NOBODY
CARED ABOUT THE THINGS HE WAS DOING TO
ME OR PUTTING ME THROUGH. THINGS WERE
JUST WAY TOO TOXIC WITH THE BOTH OF US
AND I JUST PRAYED TO GET OUT OF THE
SITUATION.

I NEEDED TO GET AWAY FROM HIM. SO I WENT
AND STAYED WITH MY GRANDMA MANDY FOR
A FEW MONTHS BUT THAT DIDN'T WORK OUT
LONG 'CAUSE SANTANA WAS STILL CALLING
AND ASKING AND NEEDING TO SEE JR.
GRANDMA MANDY DIDN'T CARE FOR HIM SO
SHE DIDN'T WANT HIM AROUND OR NOWHERE
NEAR HER HOUSE.

I FELT BAD FOR HIM CAUSE HE REALLY WAS A
GOOD FATHER WHEN IT CAME TO JR. I DIDN'T
WANT TO KEEP HIM FROM HIM. HE WILLED HIS
WAY BACK IN. NOW I'M BACK LOOKING FOR A
HOUSE. I FOUND A NICE REASONABLE HOUSE
RIGHT BEFORE THE WINTER HIT. I WASN'T IN
THE HOUSE FOR A FULL TWO MONTHS AND
HAD BEEN SCAMMED OUT OF MY MONEY. COME
TO FIND OUT THE OWNERS WEREN'T THE
OWNERS AND THE REAL OWNERS WERE IN THE
PROCESS OF SELLING THE HOUSE. SO THE
REAL OWNERS BROKE INTO THE HOUSE,

CHANGED THE LOCKS, AND DEMANDED THAT I
MOVE OUT. I CALLED THE POLICE AND MADE
POLICE REPORTS. THERE WAS NOTHING
NOBODY COULD DO IF I DIDN'T HAVE A DEED. I
PACKED MY STUFF UP AND PUT IT ALL IN
STORAGE. NOW I'M HOMELESS, SLEEPING WITH
MY BABY IN MY TRUCK OR IN A HOTEL ROOM
WHEN I COULD. MAREE WENT WITH LOUIS. I
MADE SURE WE HAD OUR EVERYDAY NEEDS AS
FAR AS MY WORK CLOTHES AND BLANKETS.
MANY NIGHTS MY YOUNGEST SON AND I
WOULD BE IN THE CAR FOR SO LONG UNTIL
THE GAS RAN OUT 'CAUSE SANTANA WAS IN
THE GAMBLING HOUSE ALL NIGHT. BY THE
TIME HE CAME OUT THERE WASN'T ANY POINT
IN GETTING A ROOM. IT WOULD BE TIME FOR
ME TO GO TO WORK. WHILE I'M WORKING,
TRYING TO SAVE UP TO MOVE AGAIN, I WOULD
LET SANTANA KEEP MY TRUCK SO HE COULD
KEEP THE BABY. IT'S GOING ON WEEK TWO, WE
ARE LIVING LIKE THIS OUT OF MY TRUCK.
SANTANA DROPPED ME OFF AT WORK BUT
WHEN IT WAS TIME FOR HIM TO COME GET ME
NO ANSWER. I'M CALLING FOR AN HOUR. HE
FINALLY CALLED OFF SOMEBODY'S PHONE AND
TOLD ME HE HAD BEEN IN A POLICE CHASE
AND CRASHED MY TRUCK WHICH WAS MY
HOME AT THE TIME AND IT WAS NOW GONE.
HE HAD WRECKED MY TRUCK. MY ONLY MEANS
OF TRANSPORTATION AND THE SAFE PLACE
FOR US TO LAY OUR HEADS. I ASKED WHERE

MY BABY WAS AND HE SAID WITH HIS MOM HE
WAS TRYING TO MAKE A MOVE SO MY BABY
COULDN'T BE WITH HIM. I HUNG UP IN HIS
FACE AND ORDERED A LYFT TO MARIE'S
HOUSE BECAUSE THAT WAS THE CLOSEST
PLACE TO MY JOB. I REALLY DIDN'T WANT TO
GO THERE CAUSE HER HOUSE KEPT GETTING
RAIDED AT THE TIME BUT I REALLY DIDN'T
HAVE A CHOICE.

WHILE I'M IN THE LYFT, TEARS ARE JUST
ROLLING DOWN MY CHEEKS AND THE DRIVER
JUST STARTS PRAYING FOR ME AND TELLING
ME HER PROBLEMS. I DON'T REMEMBER
EXACTLY WHAT SHE WAS SAYING BUT I FELT
HER SITUATION WASN'T WORSE THAN MINE. I
FINALLY GET TO MARIE'S HOUSE AND I'M JUST
CRYING AND SAYING I'M FED UP WITH HIM.
IT'S TIME TO LET HIM GO. I RELAXED A LITTLE
BECAUSE MY TAXES WERE SUPPOSED TO HIT
ANY DAY NOW. SO THAT MADE MY SITUATION
A LITTLE BETTER. WHEN THE IRS FINALLY
RELEASED MY TAXES I HAD $299 DOLLARS.
THEY HAD GARNISHED MY WHOLE CHECK FOR
STUDENT LOANS. I FELT LIKE MY WHOLE
WORLD HAD ENDED. I WAS LOST FOR DAYS.
ALL THESE THINGS HAPPENED IN ONE WEEK.

I REALLY HAD TO LEARN MY LESSON AND
STOP TAKING HIM BACK.

SANTANA BROUGHT EMOTIONAL TOXICITY. THE ARGUING AND US JUST TRYING TO MAKE SOMETHING WORK THAT WASN'T MEANT TO BE. THEN BRINGING A CHILD INTO THAT SITUATION DIDN'T HELP AT ALL. ALTHOUGH IT CALMED THINGS DOWN FOR A MOMENT IT WAS NOT IDEAL FOR WHAT I WOULD HAVE WANTED FOR MY SON. IT'S ALSO NOT WHAT I WOULD HAVE WANTED MY OLDEST SON TO SEE ME GO THROUGH. I HAD TO LET THIS SITUATION GO. I KEPT GOING BACK TO SOMETHING THAT I THOUGHT WAS COMFORTABLE FOR ME AND THE WHOLE TIME HE WAS DRAINING ME.

GHOST WAS MENTALLY TOXIC TO ME. GHOST KNEW HE HAD ME. HE KNEW HE HAD THIS HOLD ON ME THAT I COULDN'T SHAKE AND HE PLAYED ON THAT. BUT IN THE MIDST OF IT ALL, HE WAS STILL MY FRIEND. HE STILL GAVE OR POURED INTO ME IN SOME TYPE OF WAY THAT KEPT ME ENCOURAGED. THIS IS WHY IT WAS SO EASY FOR ME TO FALL BACK INTO WHAT WAS COMFORTABLE WITH HIM. I WILL NEVER FIND A BOND LIKE THIS. EVEN THOUGH OUR BOND HAS GROWN OVER THE YEARS AND WE LEARNED ABOUT EACH OTHER MORE. I WAS REALLY LEARNING NEW THINGS ABOUT

HIM THAT I THOUGHT I ALREADY KNEW.
GHOST IS LIKE AN ADDICTION I CAN'T KICK.
EVERYTHING ABOUT HIM IS SO WRONG IT
SEEMED SO RIGHT, ESPECIALLY THOSE
FOREHEAD KISSES. I ENDED UP FINDING OUT
ABOUT THE WOMEN HE DEALT WITH AND ALL
THE CHILDREN HE HAD. HE EVEN HAS ONE
THE SAME AGE AND BIRTHDATE AS MAREE
AND THAT'S JUST SOMETHING YOU DON'T SEE
ALL THE TIME. I CAN NAME A MILLION THINGS
THAT SHOULD HAVE MADE ME WALK AWAY.
BUT I'M TOO DEEP IN WITH HIM AND IT'S
HARD FOR ME TO JUST WALK AWAY.
ESPECIALLY WHEN YOU GROW TO LOVE A
PERSON I ACCEPTED HIS BAGGAGE. GHOST
WILL FOREVER BE MY GO-TO BECAUSE HE
KNOWS HE IS NOT GOOD ENOUGH FOR ME BUT
HE STILL MOTIVATES ME TO DO BETTER IN
LIFE. HE IS ALWAYS AVAILABLE FOR ME WHEN I
CALL, WHETHER IT'S A LISTENING EAR, A
SHOULDER TO CRY ON, OR A DRINK TO TURN
UP. GHOST TAUGHT ME THAT NO MATTER
WHAT YOU DO FOR A MAN, YOU CAN COOK,
CLEAN, FREAK HIM OUT, OR EVEN BUY HIM
THE WORLD AND NONE OF THAT WILL MATTER
IF HE DOESN'T WANT YOU. I HAD TO COME TO
THE REALIZATION OF MY WORTH. I FORCED
MYSELF TO LET HIM GO. I HAD TO PUT AN END
TO IT FOR THE SAKE OF BEING A MOTHER AND
FOR A BETTER MENTAL STATE FOR MY SON.

13

Life After Death

"ITS SOMETHING THAT THE PASTOR DON'T
PREACH

ITS SOMETHING THAT A TEACHER CAN'T
TEACH

WHEN WE DIE THE MONEY WE CAN'T KEEP..

BUT WE PROBABLY SPEND IT ALL CAUSE THE
PAIN AIN'T CHEAP"- KANYE WEST

I HAD TO MAKE THINGS RIGHT. I HAVE TWO
BOYS THAT ARE DEPENDING ON ME. MOVING
TO GEORGIA FOR THE FOURTH TIME,
STARTING AGAIN IN ANOTHER STATE, I
THOUGHT IT WAS THE BEST THING FOR ME
AND MY BOYS. WHEN YOU THINK OF A NEW
STATE YOU THINK IF I CAN MAKE IT IN
DETROIT, I CAN MAKE IT ANYWHERE. BUT BOY
WAS I WRONG, IT WAS HARD. I WAS IN A
BEAUTIFUL CITY BUT MY LIFE WASN'T
PROGRESSING. I WAS DOING WORSE THAN
BEFORE. I HAD TO DEPEND ON C-JAY AND HIS
WIFE TO GET AROUND BECAUSE THEY DIDN'T
WANT ME TO CHANCE IT BY DRIVING WITH NO
LICENSE. SO IT WAS HARD TRYING TO DO
THINGS ON THEIR TIME.

I COULDN'T DO ANYTHING AROUND THE CITY
IF I WANTED TO. LORD KNOWS HOW BADLY I
NEEDED A NIGHT OUT OF BAR HOPPING OR
JUST AIR. I COULDN'T GET USED TO THE CITY
OR EVEN GO OUT AND MEET DIFFERENT
PEOPLE BECAUSE I WAS STUCK IN THE HOUSE
MOST DAYS. EVERYTHING WAS AT LEAST A
HALF HOUR AWAY. MANY DAYS I WOULD GET
DISCOURAGED BECAUSE I WANTED BETTER FOR
MYSELF AND MY BOYS. I FELT AS IF I WAS
FAILING THEM AS A MOTHER BECAUSE I
DIDN'T HAVE IT TOGETHER. THERE WERE DAYS
THAT THEY WERE UNCOMFORTABLE NOT

HAVING THEIR OWN ROOM OR JUST
ADJUSTING TO C-JAY AND HIS FAMILY AND
THE WAY THEY DO THINGS. MY KIDS NEEDED
THEIR OWN SPACE AND COMFORT ZONE. BUT
OTHER THAN THAT I HAD TO GET THINGS
GOING FOR ME. I WAS WORKING THIS TIME
AROUND. C-JAY WAS HELPING ME OUT A
LITTLE MORE. I WAS EVEN STACKING MY
MONEY FOR A PLACE. I FINALLY STARTED
LOOKING FOR A HOME.

BUT I GOT SIDETRACKED ON AUGUST 14, 2019,
WHEN I GOT A CALL FROM MY SISTER MADDIE
SCREAMING AND CRYING HER HEART OUT.
"THEY GOT CHO!" "THEY JUST SHOT CHO IN
THE HEAD." "THEY CHASED HIM DOWN AND
CAUGHT HIM." THE WORST PHONE CALL IN MY
LIFE. MY LIFE HASN'T BEEN THE SAME SINCE.
CHO WAS A BIG BROTHER FROM HELL. BUT HE
WAS MY BROTHER AND LOSING HIM WILL
NEVER SIT RIGHT WITH ME. ME AND CHO'S
BATTLES START AS FAR BACK AS WHEN MY
MOMMA BROUGHT ME HOME FROM THE
HOSPITAL. THE MOMENT CHO SAW ME, HE
SLAPPED ME IN THE FACE. AS WE GREW UP WE
DIDN'T AGREE MUCH ON ANYTHING. WE
ALWAYS FOUGHT LIKE CATS AND DOGS UNLESS
IT WAS SOMEBODY ELSE TRYING TO BEEF WITH
ONE OF US THEN WE STUCK TOGETHER. HE
HAD MY BACK AND I HAD HIS. AS WE GOT

OLDER CHO WAS MORE IN THE STREETS THAN AT HOME. I ONLY SAW HIM IF WE WERE OUT IN THE HOOD OR IF HE WANTED SOMETHING LIKE MY CAR OR MONEY. HE PAID ME TO USE MY CAR AND WOULDN'T BRING IT BACK FOR DAYS AND HE WOULDN'T ANSWER THE PHONE. HE WOULD DRIVE PAST MY HOUSE AND LAUGH AT ME AND KEEP GOING JUST TO SHOW ME MY CAR WAS STILL GOOD. I WOULD HAVE TO THREATEN TO REPORT MY CAR STOLEN FOR HIM TO BRING IT BACK AND THAT SHIT DIDN'T WORK HALF OF THE TIME. I WOULD CATCH HIM AT A HOOD FUNCTION SHOOTING DICE AND HE WOULD TELL ME TO GET THE FUCK ON CAUSE HE AIN'T WANT NONE OF HIS FRIENDS TALKING TO ME. CHO LOVED HIS FRIENDS. HE WOULD DO ANYTHING FOR THEM BOYS, INCLUDING FIGHTING ME FOR THEM. CHO WAS A FINESSER AND THAT'S ALL HE KNEW. HE FINESSED HALF OF THE CITY ONE TIME AND HE GOT THE WHOLE FAMILY CHRISTMAS GIFTS.

WHEN EASTER WAS AROUND HE MADE SURE ALL THE KIDS HAD A COUPLE OF BASKETS. CHO WOULD LOOK OUT BUT YOU GOTTA GET HIM BEFORE HE GOT YOU. HE SLOWED DOWN A LITTLE WHEN HE GAVE ME MY FIRST NIECE. ONE THING IS FOR SURE HE LOVED HIS DAUGHTER AND GAVE HER THE WORLD EVERY

CHANCE HE GOT. BUT HE JUST COULDN'T GET AWAY FROM THE STREET, HE WAS TOO DEEP IN AND WASN'T ANY WAY OUT.

EVEN THROUGH ALL OF THOSE UPS AND DOWNS, THIS PHONE CALL HURT ME TO MY CORE. I THINK OUR BATTLES ARE WHAT MADE US SO CLOSE. I GOT THE CALL ABOUT CHO WHILE I WAS STILL LIVING OUT OF TOWN IN GEORGIA WITH MY DADDY. I PACKED MYSELF AND THE BOYS UP AND CAME HOME. I GOT TO DETROIT SO FAST THAT I DIDN'T HAVE TIME TO GRIEVE. AT THAT MOMENT IT WAS HARD TO BELIEVE WHAT WAS HAPPENING. I NEVER FELT THIS FEELING BEFORE. I HAD TO BE THE STRONG ONE FOR MY FAMILY. THE CRAZY THING ABOUT THIS MOMENT WAS ALL THESE TIMES WHEN I FELT LIKE MY FAMILY WASN'T REALLY THERE, WELL MY FAMILY NEEDED ME THE MOST AT THIS MOMENT. I NEVER IN MY LIFE WOULD HAVE THOUGHT I WOULD BE PLANNING MY BROTHER'S FUNERAL. I DID EVERYTHING FROM START TO FINISH AND I DON'T KNOW HOW IT HAPPENED BECAUSE I NEVER DID IT BEFORE.

AS TIME WENT ON MY DAYS GOT WORSE AND WORSE. I WOULD FIND MYSELF JUST CRYING OUT OF NOWHERE WISHING I HAD MORE TIME WITH HIM. IT WAS HARD FOR ME TO SEE MY NEPHEW OR FOR ME TO GET MY NIECE

BECAUSE SEEING THEIR FACES WAS PAINFUL. ESPECIALLY MY NIECE KNOWING THAT SHE WASN'T GONNA SEE HER FAVORITE PERSON ANYMORE. BUT I HAD TO FACE IT BECAUSE REALLY SHE COMFORTED MY PAIN. WHEN I SEE HER LITTLE FACE KNOWING THAT SHE IS A PART OF HIM. I KNOW THEY SAY WITH TIME IT WILL GET EASY BUT MY DAYS HAVE GOTTEN HARDER. THE CITY LOVED MY BROTHER AND SHOWED A LOT OF LOVE. BUT IT'S ALWAYS A FEW WHO GOT SOMETHING TO SAY, "HE WAS A BAD PERSON" OR "HE DID THIS". NO MATTER IF CHO WAS A GOOD PERSON OR BAD PERSON, HE'S STILL MY BROTHER AND I STILL LOVE HIM AFTER HIS DEATH.

14

Pain Overflow

"I'M UNSURE WHICH PAIN IS WORSE..

THE SHOCK OF WHAT HAPPENED OR THE
ACHE FOR WHAT NEVER WILL"- UNKNOWN

C-JAY HELPED ME GRIEVE THROUGH THE WHOLE PROCESS OF LOSING CHO. C-JAY WAS MY TOP PICK, MY NUMBER ONE. I'M THE FIRSTBORN OF MANY CHILDREN. I WAS A DADDY'S GIRL GROWING UP AND STILL AM. I WAS WITH C-JAY MOST OF THE TIME WHEN I WAS YOUNGER SO I KNEW ALL HIS BABY MAMAS, GIRLFRIENDS, FRIENDS, SIDE CHICKS, AND OF COURSE HIS WIFE. IF I NEEDED SOMETHING FROM C-JAY I WOULD HAVE TO WAIT OUTSIDE THE POKER HOUSE FOR HOURS BUT HE WOULD COME OUT WITH THAT MONEY. HE MADE SURE HE CAME THROUGH FOR CHRISTMAS AND MY BIRTHDAY. HE EVEN BROUGHT ME MY FIRST SHEARLING COAT AND IF YOU KNOW ANYTHING ABOUT THESE COATS, YOU KNOW I WAS KILLING EM'. C-JAY WAS A REAL DOUGHBOY BACK THEN. HE DRESSED FLY AND EVERYBODY LOVED HIM EVERYWHERE WE WENT. THE OLDER I GOT, THE MORE HE SHIFTED HIS GAME. HE MOVED TO GEORGIA, GOT MARRIED, AND JUST STARTED A NEW LIFE. HIS WIFE WAS COOL UNTIL THEY GOT MARRIED AND I SAW HER TRUE COLORS. SHE REALLY DIDN'T CARE TOO MUCH FOR OR ABOUT ME. I DEALT WITH IT BECAUSE THAT'S WHO HE CHOSE TO LOVE BUT HE WAS STILL JUST ONE PHONE CALL AWAY. HIS HOUSE WAS ALWAYS OPEN FOR ME TO STAY. I COULD TALK TO C-JAY ABOUT THE GOOD, THE BAD, OR ANYTHING. I JUST WISH

HE WAS MORE OF A FATHER THAN A BEST
FRIEND AT TIMES BUT I WOULDN'T CHANGE
OUR BOND FOR ANYTHING. HE WANTED THE
BEST FOR ME AND HE WAS SO HAPPY WHEN I
BEGAN MY LASH LINE. HE WOULD CASH APP
ME JUST BECAUSE, SAYING "HERE THIS IS FOR
YOUR LASH BUSINESS". THEN WHEN I TOLD
HIM I WAS TAKING A CLASS TO BE A
BARTENDER SO THAT I COULD START MY OWN
MOBILE BAR, HE TOLD ME TO GO FOR IT. HE
TOLD ME "I WOULD LOVE TO SEE HOW THIS
WORKS OUT."

AS I'M TELLING HIM THE NAMES I HAD IN
MIND FOR THE MOBILE BAR HE MADE A JOKE
OUT OF EVERY NAME I TOLD HIM. C-JAY'S
LAUGH WOULD MAKE ANYBODY IN THE ROOM
LAUGH. HE WAS A TRUCK DRIVER; HE HAD HIS
OWN BUSINESS AND WOULD DELIVER LOADS
ALL OVER THE COUNTRY. HE WOULD BEG ME
TO COME WORK FOR HIM BECAUSE HE KNEW I
HAD NO PROBLEM HITTING THE HIGHWAY. HE
LOVED HIS BUSINESS AND WHAT HE DID. HE
WOULD SAY "I'M MAKING THIS BUSINESS FOR
MY GRANDSONS. THIS IS GONNA BE FOR
THEM." EVERY TIME HE HAD A LOAD TO
DETROIT HE WOULD MAKE HIS WAY TO ME
AND STAY WITH ME. HE ALWAYS REMINDED ME
I WAS A SURVIVOR AND I WAS STRONG. I
WOULD TALK TO MY DAD ALMOST EVERY DAY

FOR HOURS. WHEN WE DIDN'T HEAR FROM
EACH OTHER FOR A WEEK OR SO IT WAS ODD.
BUT OUR VERY LAST CONVERSATION WE HAD
WAS WHEN HE CALLED ME LIKE "DANG YOU
DON'T LOVE YOUR DADDY NO MORE. YOU ACT
LIKE ME AND YO MOMMA OWE YOU
SOMETHING." MY RESPONSE WAS, "NO, DON'T
NOBODY OWE ME ANYTHING. I GOT THIS FAR
ON MY OWN. I'M JUST TRYING TO GET MY LIFE
TOGETHER." HE SAID, "WELL I'M IN THE CITY
DROPPING OFF A LOAD AND I WANT TO SEE
YOU." I SAID "OK," HE SAID, "IMA MEET YOU
LATER BEFORE YOU GO TO WORK."

HE NEVER CALLED BACK OR MET ME LATER
THAT NIGHT. I GOT A CALL AT FIVE IN THE
MORNING FROM MY GRANDAD SPEEDY SAYING
MY DAD WAS GONE. AFTER THAT MY LIFE
CHANGED FOREVER. C-JAY HAD BEEN IN A BAD
CAR ACCIDENT ON THE 94 FREEWAY AND WAS
PRONOUNCED DEAD WHEN HE ARRIVED AT
THE HOSPITAL. I WAS DEVASTATED. I JUST
COULDN'T BELIEVE IT. I FELT KNOTS IN MY
STOMACH. I STILL HAVE THEM TO THIS DAY
EVERY TIME I THINK ABOUT MY DAD. I FELT SO
EMPTY, HURT, FRUSTRATED, AND LOST. IT WAS
A DIFFERENT PAIN FROM CHO . I DIDN'T
UNDERSTAND WHY A NICE GUY WHO LOVED
EVERYBODY AND WORKED HARD FOR HIS
FAMILY WAS HERE TODAY, GONE TOMORROW. I

WANTED TO GIVE UP MY LIFE. THINGS STARTED TO GET SCARY FOR ME. I HAD TO SNAP BACK TO REALITY. I HAVE MY BOYS WHO DEPEND ON ME. SO I HAD TO SHAKE IT OFF. I TURNED TO GOD AND PRAYED FOR STRENGTH AND GUIDANCE BECAUSE THIS IS A PAIN I KNEW I WOULD HAVE TO LIVE WITH FOR THE REST OF MY LIFE. IT'S HARD AND MY DAYS GET HARDER AS TIME GOES ON. IT'S SO MUCH I WANT TO CALL AND TALK TO HIM ABOUT. SO MANY PLANS I NEEDED HIM TO SEE ME THROUGH. HE SAW THE DRIVE IN ME BREWING WITH THE CLASSES I WAS TAKING AND THE MOVES I WAS MAKING. BUT HE DIDN'T GET TO SEE THE RESULTS. HE DIDN'T GET TO SEE HOW THE THINGS I WENT THROUGH MADE ME STRONGER AND I WAS USING THE HUSTLE THAT WAS JUST IN ME TO MAKE MY SITUATION BETTER. THROUGH EVERYTHING, I NEVER BLAMED ANYONE FOR ANYTHING I WENT THROUGH. I TOOK THE LICKS ON THE CHIN AND HE SAW THAT BUT THERE'S ANOTHER SIDE TO THAT. I HATE HE'S NOT HERE TO SEE THE FRUITS OF MY LABOR BUT I'M FOREVER GRATEFUL THAT HE LEFT ME WITH SIBLINGS KERMAN, KARRON, MOO, AND TEJA. LOSING HIM MADE US GET CLOSER AND MADE OUR BONDS STRONGER. WE LIVE THROUGH HIM. HE DEFINITELY LEFT A MARK ON ALL OF US. WE ALL GOT HIS LAUGH. AND HE FOR SURE GAVE ME HIS SMILE.

LOSING YOU HAS BEEN THE WORST PAIN. MY
PAIN KEEPS OVERFLOWING.

DAD, I REALLY WISH WE HAD EXTRA TIME
TOGETHER.

I'LL NEVER GET TO EXPERIENCE THAT
DADDY-DAUGHTER DANCE.

15

The Reason I Smile

"FOR, AFTER ALL, YOU DO GROW UP, YOU DO OUTGROW YOUR IDEALS, WHICH TURN TO DUST AND ASHES,

WHICH ARE SHATTERED INTO FRAGMENTS; AND YOU HAVE NO OTHER LIFE,

SO YOU JUST HAVE TO BUILD ONE UP OUT OF THOSE FRAGMENTS"- FYODOR DOSTOYEVSKY

NOW I'M ADJUSTING MY CROWN. I'M JUST A GIRL FROM THE D THAT TURNED MY STRUGGLE AND FAILURE INTO SUCCESS. I NEVER HAD ANY ROLE MODEL OR SOMEONE TO LOOK UP TO. SO I'M MORE DETERMINED THAN EVER TO BE SOMEBODY. SOMETIMES THE GIRL I USED TO BE, APPEARS IN MY HEAD BUT THEN I HAVE TO REMIND MYSELF WHO I AM TODAY. THROUGH IT ALL, I'LL NEVER FORGET WHERE I CAME FROM. IT'S LIKE I WOULD START SOMETHING AND NEVER FINISH BUT HERE I AM TODAY TELLING MY STORY. I LEARNED PEOPLE ARE GOING TO TALK ABOUT YOU WHETHER YOU ARE DOING GOOD OR BAD. SO JUST DO WHAT'S BEST FOR YOU AND BE YOURSELF WHILE DOING IT. THE GROWTH AND HEALING PROCESS IS HARD BUT IT'S IMPORTANT FOR THE FUTURE. I DIDN'T COME FROM A FAMILY OF WEALTH NOR DID I HAVE AN EXTRA PUSH OR A HANDOUT FROM A MAN. IF YOU TRULY READ THROUGH EVERY SITUATION I WAS IN WITH THESE GUYS OF MY PAST EVEN WHEN THEY WERE GIVING ME MONEY OR CARS OR WHATEVER WHEN I LOST STUFF I LOST IT ALL. I ALWAYS ENDED UP BACK AT SQUARE ONE. BUT THAT'S BECAUSE I REALLY BELIEVE I WASN'T SUPPOSED TO HAVE IT THAT WAY. SO NOW GOD IS GIVING ME EVERYTHING TENFOLD BECAUSE I'M MAKING AN EFFORT TO DO THINGS THE RIGHT WAY.

MY WAY. EVERYTHING I HAVE, I BUILT ON MY OWN, STRAIGHT OUT OF THE MUD. I'M REALLY AFRAID TO RETURN TO THOSE HOMELESS DAYS. SO I HUSTLE A LITTLE HARDER THAN OTHERS, LEARN AS I GROW AND ALL I SEE IS THE TOP FOR ME. I NEED HEALING AND I'M STILL LEARNING TO LOVE MYSELF AND THAT'S OKAY.

NOW I'M THIRTY YEARS OLD, I'M ALL FOR MYSELF. I LOVE MYSELF MORE THAN ANYTHING IN THIS WORLD. I DIDN'T THINK I WOULD MAKE IT THIS FAR. I'M DOING BETTER THAN A LOT OF PEOPLE THAT SAID I WOULDN'T AMOUNT TO ANYTHING. I HAVE MY OWN MOBILE BAR BUSINESS THAT I STARTED THIS YEAR 2022 AND IT'S BEEN DOING GREAT FOR ME. ESPECIALLY FOR IT TO ONLY BE MY FIRST YEAR. I SELL THE BEST MINK LASHES AND SEX TOYS IN THE CITY. I JUST PURCHASED MY FIRST LASH VENDING MACHINE. I'M ALSO IN THE PROCESS OF BECOMING A NEW HOMEOWNER. ALL OF THESE THINGS THAT ARE HAPPENING IN MY LIFE NOW ARE FROM STANDING ON THE FOUNDATION THAT WAS LAID IN THE EARLY YEARS OF MY LIFE. NO MATTER HOW HARD THE PROCESS STARTS OFF YOU HAVE TO LEARN HOW TO KEEP MOVING BECAUSE IT'S ALL A JOURNEY. THROUGH THIS JOURNEY CALLED LIFE, I WILL ALWAYS KEEP A

SMILE ON MY FACE AND KEEP GOING HARD
FOR MY BOYS. I OWE THEM THE WORLD. A LOT
OF THESE STRUGGLES I'VE BEEN THROUGH
MADE ME HUMBLE BUT THEY ALSO LIT A FIRE
IN ME. I DIDN'T HAVE TIME TO SIT DOWN ON
MYSELF BECAUSE I HAD MY BOYS DEPENDING
ON ME. WITH THEM DEPENDING ON ME AND
GOD WALKING WITH ME I COULDN'T LOSE.

IN LIFE, THERE WILL BE MANY OBSTACLES BUT
IT'S UP TO YOU TO NEVER GIVE UP.
EVERYBODY HAS A STORY TO TELL, MINE'S
JUST A LITTLE DIFFERENT. I JUST WORE MY
PAIN DIFFERENTLY. I DEALT WITH MANY
THINGS MENTALLY PHYSICALLY, FINANCIALLY,
AND EMOTIONALLY. DEPRESSION, LOW
SELF-ESTEEM YOU NAME IT, BUT I HID IT ALL
INSIDE. I HAVE BEEN BETRAYED PLENTY OF
TIMES AND COUNTED OUT MANY DAYS
BECAUSE PEOPLE DIDN'T HAVE THAT FAITH IN
ME. BUT IF YOU DON'T HAVE FAITH AND LOVE
YOURSELF, WHO ELSE WILL? I WAS RAISED ON
SURVIVAL. THAT'S WHY I'M SO STRONG TODAY.
I LOST IT ALL AND GOT IT BACK MORE TIMES
THAN I CAN COUNT. THAT'S WHAT MAKES ME
THE BOSS THAT I AM.

I PROBABLY RUFFLED A LOT OF FEATHERS AND
BEAT A LOT OF ASS. BUT ALL OF THAT WAS ME

GROWING THROUGH MY PROCESS. THAT YOUNG GIRL IS NOW A WOMAN AND I PLAN TO CONTINUE TO POUR INTO THIS WOMAN AND GIVE NOT ONLY MY BOYS EVERYTHING THAT THEY DESERVE BUT MYSELF AS WELL. I DESERVE ALL THE GOOD THAT IS HAPPENING AND ALL THE GOOD THAT WILL COME. I'VE CRIED FOR IT, I'VE BEEN HOMELESS FOR IT. I'VE MADE MISTAKES FOR IT BUT MOST IMPORTANTLY I'VE PRAYED FOR IT. I'M FOREVER HUMBLE AND BLESSED. WHETHER TAKING A STEP INTO A CHURCH OR NOT- THE RELATIONSHIP I HAVE WITH GOD IS SUPER REAL. I KNOW HE GOT ME BECAUSE I KNOW WHERE I COME FROM. AS FOR LOVE, I AM JUST GONNA HAVE TO LEAVE IT IN THE HANDS OF GOD. HE WILL COME ALONG WHEN IT'S TIME. GOD IS REAL, THAT'S WHY I'M WHERE I AM TODAY. ON THE ROAD TO SUCCESS. I'M JUST PLAYING THE HAND I WAS DEALT. I'VE ALWAYS WORN MY STRUGGLE WITH A SMILE AND IN SPITE OF ALL THAT PAIN, I'LL KEEP SMILING.

 I JUST WANT TO BE A BLESSING TO OTHERS AND ENCOURAGE THEM TO DO WHATEVER IT IS IN LIFE. WORK HARD, STAY CONSISTENT, AND HAVE A LITTLE PATIENCE. KEEP PUSHING AND NEVER CARE WHAT OTHERS THINK OF YOU. PUT GOD FIRST IN EVERYTHING YOU DO

AND AGAIN REMEMBER TO ALWAYS BE
YOURSELF. THANKS AGAIN TO EVERYONE
THAT SUPPORTS ME.

IN LOVING MEMORY OF

CLARA & RONALD ADAMS

RODNEY ADAMS

07/18/1990 - 08/14/2019

CALVIN MALLETT JR.

01/28/1974 - 09/18/2021

Copyright © 2022 by Cymone Adams

TyneBell Publishing, 2022

CPSIA information can be obtained
at www.ICGtesting.com
Printed in the USA
BVHW032337171122
652258BV00011B/123